STOP ME IF YOU'VE READ THIS ONE

Prairie Lite

WINNER OF TWO RITA® AWARDS FROM
ROMANCE WRITERS OF AMERICA FOR BEST REGENCY OF THE YEAR

CARLA KELLY

STOP ME IF YOU'VE READ THIS ONE
Prairie Lite

PLAIN SIGHT PUBLISHING
AN IMPRINT OF CEDAR FORT, INC.
SPRINGVILLE, UTAH

© 2013 Carla Kelly

All rights reserved.

No part of this book may be reproduced in any form whatsoever, whether by graphic, visual, electronic, film, microfilm, tape recording, or any other means, without prior written permission of the publisher, except in the case of brief passages embodied in critical reviews and articles. The views expressed within this work are the sole responsibility of the author and do not necessarily reflect the position of Cedar Fort, Inc., or any other entity. Permission for the use of sources, graphics, or photos is also solely the responsibility of the author.

ISBN 13: 978-1-4621-1191-6

Reprinted with permission from Horizon Publications and the *Valley City Times-Record*

Published by Plain Sight Publishing, an imprint of Cedar Fort, Inc.
2373 W. 700 S. Springville, UT 84663
Distributed by Cedar Fort, Inc., www.cedarfort.com

LIBRARY OF CONGRESS CATALOGING-IN-PUBLICATION DATA

Kelly, Carla, author.
 [Essays. Selections]
 Stop me if you've read this one / Carla Kelly.
    pages cm
 Includes bibliographical references and index.
 Summary: Collection of columns written for the Valley City Times-Record (Valley City, North Dakota) from 2004 to 2008.
 ISBN 978-1-4621-1191-6 (alk. paper)
 1. Essays. I. Title.

PS3561.E3928S76 2013
814'.54--dc23

2012050062

Cover design by Angela D. Olsen
Cover design © 2012 by Lyle Mortimer
Edited and typeset by Whitney A. Lindsley

Printed in the United States of America

10 9 8 7 6 5 4 3 2 1

To my North Dakota fans,
who made my job so easy.

Thanks.

Also by Carla Kelly

Fiction

Daughter of Fortune
Summer Campaign
Miss Chartley's Guided Tour
Marian's Christmas Wish
Mrs. McVinnie's London Season
Libby's London Merchant
Miss Grimsley's Oxford Career
Miss Billings Treads the Boards
Mrs. Drew Plays Her Hand
Reforming Lord Ragsdale
Miss Whittier Makes a List
The Lady's Companion
With This Ring
Miss Milton Speaks Her Mind
One Good Turn
The Wedding Journey
Here's to the Ladies: Stories of the Frontier Army
Beau Crusoe
Marrying the Captain
The Surgeon's Lady
Marrying the Royal Marine
The Admiral's Penniless Bride
Borrowed Light
Coming Home for Christmas: Three Holiday Stories
Enduring Light
Marriage of Mercy
My Loving Vigil Keeping
Her Hesitant Heart

Nonfiction

On the Upper Missouri: The Journal of Rudolph Friedrich Kurz
Fort Buford: Sentinel at the Confluence

CONTENTS

INTRODUCTION ix
WAR. 1
PLACES AND MOVING 21
WRITING AND EDUCATION. 55
HISTORY AND TRADITION. 93
FAMILY AND EVERYDAY LIFE 151
ABOUT THE AUTHOR. 195

INTRODUCTION

In *The Importance of Being Earnest*, Oscar Wilde's brilliant comedy, the shrewdly naïve Cecily Cardew tells Algernon Moncrieff about her diary: "You see, it is simply a very young girl's record of her own thoughts and impressions, and consequently meant for publication."

That pretty much sums up *Stop Me If You've Read This One: Prairie Lite*. Between 2005 and 2008. I was a reporter for a daily metropolitan newspaper—whoa, back up, delete. That's Superman, and I most emphatically am not Superman, the caped avenger. Valley City, North Dakota, is not Metropolis.

I was a reporter for the Valley City *Times-Record*, a small daily newspaper in a town on the prairie. We were an afternoon paper, so I arrived at the newspaper office at 0-dawn o'clock, put the finishing touches on my articles, edited others' articles, and once a week put together my own arts and entertainment page.

Along the way, I convinced the editor that I could write a weekly column. It would be roughly 750 words of whatever I thought folks in Valley City might want to read. I named it "Prairie Lite," because I knew it would be humorous.

It became more than just humorous. "Prairie Lite" was at times quite serious. I introduced the newspapers to a cast of characters from my life: close family, National Park Service rangers (I was one), cousins, exotic places where life took me as the daughter of a US Navy officer, fraught and/or funny situations; you name it, I wrote 750–800 words about it. That's the fun of column writing.

As it turned out, readers embraced the column, and me. I'm no extrovert; I leave that to my husband, Martin Kelly. At the time, he was director of theatre at Valley City State University, and everyone knew him. Through the column, they came to know me.

I think what they really came to know was life: its humor, trauma, and pivotal moments, things we all share because we're part of the human family. I think readers saw themselves. One reader told me that my columns made him think about his own life, with its ups and downs, triumphs and tragedies.

Some of these columns won awards from the North Dakota Newspaper Association, which confirmed to me that others saw themselves in those weekly 750 words. Through the voodoo of the Internet, I developed a readership that spanned the globe.

I had fun along the way. At the end of each year, I packaged a year's work of columns in a spiral-bound book and sent it to close friends and relatives. Some 30 people have those volumes.

And that was that, or so I thought. After Martin retired and we moved to Wellington, Utah, I continued writing novels, something I've done successfully since 1984. I started writing for Cedar Fort, a nimble press located in Springville, Utah. We're having some good times there.

One day last year, I mailed two of my "Prairie Lites" to Jennifer Fielding, then an acquisitions editor for Cedar Fort. We had been e-mailing back and forth about some subject or other, and I sent those to her just to illustrate the issue.

According to Jennifer, she set the two columns on her desk, where Lyle Mortimer, Cedar Fort publisher, saw them. He liked them, asked about them, and thought maybe Cedar Fort should publish the whole *oeuvre* (that's French for "lame-brained, crackpot stuff").

Thank you, Horizon Publications, Inc., for giving me permission to publish these columns, which originally appeared in the Valley City *Times-Record*.

Here they are. Bear in mind that they were written between 2004 and 2009. In our fast-moving century, that might render some columns a bit quaint. Others are spot on and up to date, because the human condition seems to muddle along in much the same manner from century to century.

You'll meet my folks, Dot and Casey Baier; my children, Jeremy, Mary Ruth, Sam, Sarah, and Liz; my husband, Martin; my super-sisters, Wanda Lynn and Karen; my Trask cousins and their parents; ranger friends; and friends in general. You'll also get a glimpse into a historian's brain, because that is what I am. Oh, a novelist, too, and we do think differently. You'll meet the fluffy woman who stammers, is a Mormon, has flat feet, makes mistakes of the head-slapping variety, and sees life from a slightly skewed perspective.

What you'll probably end up doing is thinking about your own life and its adventures. If you do, I've succeeded with "Prairie Lite."

I'll finish where I began, with a quote from Cecily Cardew, speaking of her diary: "When it appears in volume form I hope you will order a copy."

Carla Kelly
Wellington, Utah

P.S. Kindly note that this Introduction is about 780 words. That was unintentional, but it is the length of a typical column. Old habits die hard.

WAR

JANUARY 6, 2005

THE VIEW FROM HERE

North Dakotans must be the most optimistic people in America. I think it's contagious.

Who else would go outside when it was clear, and nine below, and say, "What a beautiful day!" Anyone from a warmer state (pick any 47 or so) overhearing that Northern Plains euphoria would probably start backing away slowly, speaking in soothing tones, and avoiding eye contact.

We're *not* crazy. Nine below and clear out *is* beautiful, if the day before was fifteen below, snowing and blowing, and preceded by an ice storm that even froze the garden gnome. Is it more than optimism, or do we understand perspective better than any other people?

My initial North Dakota dose of perspective came in 1997, my first autumn here. It was October, and change was in the air. One morning I heard geese honking overhead. I quickly realized that those birds Knew Something: winter was coming. Listening to those birds honk and point their formations toward sandy beaches was the most melancholy sound I've ever heard. Winter was coming, with its cold, dark, and snow. I'll never forget how sad that sound made me feel.

Sure enough, winter was all of the above. Then sometime in March, when the snow was still deep, I heard that same honking overhead. The birds were back! Spring was coming. In an emotional rush that is hard to describe, I was happier than I had been in a long while. Same sound, same birds: totally different emotional reaction. Perspective.

That was the first year that Groundhog Day actually meant something. When you're from warmer parts of the US and Punxsutawney Phil sees his shadow on February 2, that means six more weeks of winter. Up to or around March 15, it's going to snow and blow, so forget an early spring. Inhabitants of wimpy states feel sad and trembly-mouthed.

Not here. Woo-hoo! Only six more weeks of winter! When Ol' Phil sees his rodent shadow, it's time to break out the party hats and the chip dip. In North Dakota, only six more weeks of winter sounds like heaven. See? Perspective.

I got a more significant dose of perspective—one I never forgot—when I was seven years old. In 1954, my dad—a career Navy man—got orders to Japan. It was nine years after the end of World War II. Yokohama was a bustling city rising from the ashes like that cool bird nobody can spell, but there were still acres of bombed and burned-out rubble.

I was in the second grade in nearby Yokosuka, a US Navy base that during the war was a Japanese naval base. It was the height of the Cold War in 1954, and we were all familiar with air raid drills. During school, when the siren sounded for a drill, we were marched across the street and into the caves. We stayed there until the all clear, then returned to class.

Because of my father's military connection and my early interest in history, I already knew something about World War II. When I stood there with my classmates in that dark cave and waited for the all clear, I realized that Japanese school children my age must have hid out there nine years ago, when the American enemy bombed "their" navy base. After the cave, I had a whole different perspective on war, because I knew what it felt like to literally stand in someone else's shoes.

This childhood perspective never gave me any anxiety about our role in the war against Japan. They were the aggressors, and some wars are meant to be fought. What it did give me was a global outlook that still makes me try to see more than one side of any issue, whether I want to or not. For example, once a mighty nation tried to force its principles, government, and economics on some folks who chose to fight instead. We called it the American Revolution. On the Arab Street, I might be describing the current war in Iraq.

Perspective is a powerful thing. It can make us happy or sad, brave or afraid. Sometimes it even helps us think.

APRIL 7, 2005

WISH YOU WERE HERE

The bluebonnets are blooming in Texas now, and I wish I were there. You see bluebonnets mixed in with scarlet Indian paintbrush, shy lantana, yellow Mexican Hat, and yucca. Fields of flowers go on for miles, and I do not exaggerate. There is no more beautiful place on earth than Texas when the flowers bloom.

Invariably I think of John Baker, son of Texas, when the bluebonnets march across the state. I used to think of John with sadness, but after my visit to the Vietnam Memorial in Washington, DC, in 2000, I'm not so sad.

He was Baker and I was Baier then, so in some classes where the teachers sat students alphabetically, he sat behind me. John ran around with the automotive guys, and I hung out with the journalists, so we didn't have a lot in common. It was one of those high school friendships where I know you and you know me, and we laugh together now and then, but nothing more. He was a nice guy.

We were in the class of 1965, which pretty much found itself in Vietnam. I went to college, and John went to war. He was killed in 1967, the first one I knew who died there in that jungle so far from South Texas. Years have passed, but I still feel a serious pang when I think about that. More than a pang, I guess. Pangs don't make computer keys blurry.

Time passed. I married, and Martin and I moved to Brooklyn, New York, so he could work on a graduate degree. New York may be the center of the world to many people, but can I tell you how many times I stood at the window and faced myself in a southwesterly direction, wishing I could see Texas in the spring?

One day along about this time of year, another friend of mine from Texas sent me a bluebonnet in a letter. The colors had faded, but not entirely. There was still that little spark of blue. I pressed the flower between plastic sheeting to preserve it.

Right around the time I received the flower, the Vietnam War Memorial was under construction. Soon it would have all those names inscribed of men and women who gave everything they possessed for the benefit of others. John Baker would be there. Thirty years ago in New York City, I promised myself that someday I would get that bluebonnet to John.

More years went by. We moved west, much farther from the Wall. I kept the bluebonnet in my jewelry box, and I must admit it started to mock me. I had promised I would get that flower to John, and there it was in Wyoming, then Utah, then Missouri, then Louisiana, then North Dakota.

In 2000, I was invited to participate in a project researching the history of the confluence of the Missouri and Yellowstone Rivers. This would involve several trips to the National Archives in Washington, DC. I signed on with pleasure, partly because I really believed in the project and love historical research, and partly because I knew I could get that bluebonnet to John.

And I did. Before flying back to North Dakota after a week at the National Archives, I went to the Wall. A drizzly rain was falling. One of the helpful guides there showed me precisely where John's name was located. John was at a height I could reach, so I smoothed my finger across his name.

Wall watchers say that men and women approach those names differently. Vets often will cover a name with their hand, as though to blot out that the death happened or that they were there to witness it. Women touch the name, as though caressing it. I did precisely that. I remember thinking, "Oh, John, there you are."

I left the bluebonnet at the Wall, as I had promised I would, thirty years before. I stood there looking at his name, and back at my reflection in the Wall, so grateful to have had the opportunity to leave a bluebonnet for one of Texas's modest, polite, kind, ordinary sons.

John, they bloom for you.

APRIL 28, 2005

GETTING TO KNOW YOU

I just returned from Whidbey Island, Washington, where my folks celebrated their 60th wedding anniversary. Dad will be 82 on May 16. He's cagey about what he tells me and my two sisters concerning his health. He never complains, even though he could. When we ask how he's doing, he says, "We're still on this side of the daisies, and buying green bananas."

He's sharp and witty, and after all these years, I wish I knew him better. I think his navy career made him a little remote to his three daughters. During my childhood, he was frequently gone, involved in war or peacekeeping.

His squadron—he was in naval aviation—often had sea duty for generous hunks of time. When he and Mom lived in the Aleutian Islands, we never knew what his actual duties were, because he wasn't allowed to tell us.

I missed him; we all did. Dad looks a great deal like the actor Glenn Ford, who'll be 88 on May 1. We rarely missed a Glenn Ford movie, especially when Ford played a navy man. It was like seeing Dad on the big screen.

I always wanted to know more about Dad's years in the South Pacific during World War II. He served on Guadalcanal and in the Fiji and Russell islands. Dad never liked to talk about the war, so I only heard bits and snatches of his experiences.

That changed in the summer of 1977, when I got a glimpse of my father that I cherish.

That was the summer the movie *Midway* came out. The battle for Midway Island took place June 4–7, 1942, and stopped the Japanese advance in the Pacific. Aside from a tacked-on love story, *Midway* was a good flick, featuring real combat footage that was colorized.

I saw the movie. When my folks came to visit us that summer, it was fresh in my mind. I knew better than to expect Dad to talk about his own war experiences, so I didn't ask him anything.

At least I didn't until one midnight, when he and I were the only ones still awake. I was pitting cherries to bottle in the morning, and he was helping. We chatted about the movie (he had seen it earlier) and then branched out into the general stupidity of war, blah, blah, blah.

Then I asked him kind of casually: "Dad, did the strangeness of war ever get to you?"

He actually answered me. "Three times," he said. I wanted to whip out my notebook, but I knew he would clam up if I did. I listened, and I never forgot.

"The first time was on Guadalcanal," he said. The Marines had taken an enemy soldier alive, a real rarity, since the Japanese preferred suicide to surrender. Dad went to look at the POW.

"It was the monsoon season," Dad said, "and he was just squatting there in the rain, inside a wire fence. I asked myself, 'What's a Wyoming boy like me doing here in the South Pacific?'"

The second time was on a carrier. A fighter plane from Dad's squadron had been catapulted off, but some malfunction caused it to slam back onto the deck, where it exploded. "I lost friends in that plane," Dad said as he kept on pitting cherries.

The third time was during his Vietnam tour of duty at Yankee Station, located in the Gulf of Tonkin. He was officer on deck, twelve hours on, and twelve off—pretty strenuous duty for a guy about to retire.

"Every time pilots found a target in Vietnam, they had to get permission to bomb from Washington, DC." Dad shook his head. "That's no way to run a war."

Three incidents: three little glimpses into my father's heart. I'm thinking of this now, because when I left Whidbey Island, Dad gave me his coin collection. It's no formal collection, just a box containing coins he acquired from years of overseas assignments and civilian travel.

The coin I already cherish is a silver one from Fiji, minted in 1942, with a hole drilled through it. Dad must have worn that during his World War II years. Was it for good luck? He's still buying green bananas, so I guess it worked.

As soon as I can find a chain, that coin is going around my neck. Anchors aweigh, Dad. And same to you, Glenn Ford.

JUNE 2, 2005

THE WRITE-EST THING I EVER DID

With Memorial Day, Vietnam is on my mind.

In the summer of 1966, I worked as a cashier at the Navy Exchange on Adak in the Aleutian Islands, a great job. There was no downside to admiring scores—nay, hundreds—of Navy guys.

One of them was Harold Suess. Harold was a Seabee, one of the Navy's construction battalion guys who can do just about anything. Harold worked in the warehouse, and since I had to stock shelves, I often saw him there. (Amazing how many trips I had to make to the warehouse . . .)

Harold was a solid, corn-fed guy from Moberly, Missouri: blond and blue-eyed, and handsome. We hit it off well but, ironically, didn't date until summer was almost over. I went back to college, and he went to Vietnam. I promised to write.

I wrote Harold once a week. His letters came regularly from Da Nang and were often about funny stuff that happened. Sometimes he'd gripe; sometimes he'd write about the tougher stuff. At Christmas he sent me a lovely pearl necklace. Tucked in the case is a note I still keep: "All my love, Harold. Too bad I can't be there to give these to you."

Something happened after Christmas. It wasn't just the lovely gift; I'd gotten nice things before. Maybe it was the fact that the war news kept getting worse and worse. Whatever it was, I started writing to Harold every day. I heard from him nearly every week. When I didn't, I worried. It got so that I just lived for those white envelopes with the red and blue borders. Somehow in my mind I knew that if I got a letter, Harold had to be alive. Never mind that he could have died after he mailed the letter. He was alive and that's all there was to it. I don't think it was love, because I was seeing someone else. I'm not sure what it was. Somehow in my mind, my endless chain of letters was a weird kind of talisman keeping him—willing him—alive. I can't explain it.

I got engaged in the fall of 1967, about the time Harold came home. He called me when he got to San Francisco, and I broke the news to him over the phone. I know he was disappointed, but he still wanted to see me.

I met him in Salt Lake City about a week later, and we had a nice visit. He looked good, if a little thinner. He told me of his plans, and I wished him well. He had to catch a plane, and I had to get back to school. Before he kissed me and said good-bye, he thanked me for all those letters. I never forgot what he said: "Carla, I always knew that no matter what happened, I would have a letter from you. You never let me down. Every single mail call, there were letters."

Fast forward now to Louisiana in February 1991. I had lost track of Harold since 1967, and wondered about him. Remembering Moberly, I called the high school there. By coincidence, the woman I talked to happened to be Harold's cousin. She gave me his address in Maryland, and I sent him a birthday card.

Less than a week later, Harold called. For the next hour or two, we caught up on 24 years. He'd stayed in the Navy and was currently working at Camp David, Maryland (with stories to tell about presidential visits).

Life had been tough after Vietnam. His own sister, antiwar to the core, called him a baby killer and refused to see him. A marriage had failed, but he was happily married now to a nurse, and they were planning to retire in a few years to her home in Trumansburg, New York.

Partway through our conversation, I told him I was smiling so big that my face hurt. He said the same thing was happening to him on the other end of the line.

I haven't heard from Harold in a year or two, so I sent him a letter last week, which included my e-mail address. I hope he writes. There was a time during a bad time when he needed me, and I needed him. It's an interesting bond that I wouldn't trade for anything.

I kept his letters. I always will.

JANUARY 12, 2006

MY HEROES HAVE ALWAYS BEEN SOLDIERS

One of my heroes died last week. You may have read of his death. If you have kids in the market for a role model, he'll do.

Hugh Thompson Jr. was the helicopter pilot, who, when coming upon the slaughter of Vietnamese civilians by US Army troops at My Lai, set down his helicopter between the soldier and civilians. He jumped out of his OH-23 and ordered Lieutenant Stephen Brooks, a superior officer, to stop.

Thompson also commanded his two gunners to shoot any soldier who refused his orders to stop firing.

Through Thompson's efforts, other helicopters in the vicinity landed and evacuated wounded Vietnamese. As Thompson was flying out, gunner Glenn Andreotta noticed movement in that infamous ditch of dead civilians. Thompson landed his helicopter again so Andreotta could pull out eight-year-old Do Hoa and take him to a hospital.

It's shameful, but probably true, that Thompson was hazed by other GIs resentful of the negative publicity the incident heaped on the army. He was already serving a dangerous mission when he happened upon My Lai. Thompson and his crew were attached to Task Force Barker, whose job it was to fly low and draw enemy fire, in order to establish the location of enemy troops.

Rumor said Thompson was kept on that mission far beyond any requirements as punishment for his "interference." Thompson was shot down five times, and seriously injured the last time. He lived, though, and eventually settled in Louisiana.

Thirty years after My Lai, Thompson, Andreotta, and door-gunner Lawrence Colburn were awarded the Soldier's Medal for their heroism at My Lai. The Soldier's Medal is the highest honor the army can give for bravery not involving direct contact with the enemy.

Maybe I shouldn't quibble, but I would have given them the Congressional Medal of Honor for bravery in the face of the enemy, even though the enemy in this case was the US Army. Wrong is wrong, after all.

Andreotta's family collected his medal for him in 1998. He had died in battle three weeks after My Lai.

That same year, the two surviving warriors returned to My Lai. They dedicated an elementary school there and met with Do Hoa, now a grown man and alive because a helicopter crew wasn't afraid to do the right thing.

When I read about Thompson, I thought of General George Thomas, a remarkable general in the Union army who served with the Army of the Cumberland. A Southerner married to a woman from the North, Thomas chose to remain with the Union, even when his friends Lee, Longstreet, Johnston, and Hardee offered their services to the Confederate States of America.

Thomas was regarded with some suspicion, but his successful soldiering for the Union cause was undeniable. His soldiers called him "Pap" Thomas, a telling sign of the affection they had for him.

Thomas used to irritate U. S. Grant because he was so methodical, preferring to get every duck in a row before he attacked. It's hardly surprising that today he's best remembered as a master of logistics.

Thomas's method paid off. Even as Grant was sending furious telegrams to him in Nashville in late 1864, demanding that he attack Texan John Bell Hood and his army, Thomas refused to budge until ready. When he did move, Thomas slammed into Hood's army like a battering ram.

The Battle of Nashville is the only instance in the Civil War where an army was totally destroyed. Hood's forces never fought again.

But mostly I remember Thomas as the "Rock of Chickamauga." When Thomas's superior, General William Rosecrans, ran from the battlefield, Thomas calmly rallied his troops and held. And held, earning himself that nickname.

Any historian knows the most interesting military history happens when everything is going wrong, whether at My Lai or Chickamauga. It's when every instinct in a soldier's body is screaming, "Run the other way," that courage blooms.

Thomas Paine put it well in his pamphlet *The Crisis*. For every "summer soldier and sunshine patriot," there is the opposite: ". . . but he that stands it now, deserves the love and thanks of men and women."

Scots have a dirge called "Flowers of the Forest" they play when remembering the honored dead. I played it Sunday afternoon for Hugh Thompson.

JANUARY 12, 2006

IT AIN'T HEAVY; IT'S JUST UGLY

I hate my coat. This is a problem because it's only January, and here in North Dakota, spring won't arrive for another six months.

I knew this was coming. I hated the same coat by the end of winter last year, but the darned thing refused to wear out. I can't afford a new one. Even if I could, such wild extravagance would send all my Scots ancestors spinning in their narrow, frugal graves.

I bought the thing in December of 2000 because I was heading to Washington, DC, for research, and wanted a lighter coat for the warmer weather. I somehow thought denim would be lighter. It wasn't.

In Washington, the denim coat didn't allow me to blend in with the natives, all of whom wore black. You'd have thought DC was a Johnny Cash convention with lobbyists. The other project researcher was a professor from NDSU, and he wore his parka. We probably looked like Jean and Jerry Lundegaard from the movie *Fargo*.

If I'd had to wear that coat all year around, I would have worn it out sooner and replaced it. I've thought about just leaving my coat somewhere, but it would probably come home like a cat, slinking up the driveway and flopping down on the porch.

Maybe I should have named my coat. That simple act might have increased my affection. Years ago, my husband bought a used Buick. It was green and huge. We had five children; I think, in a pinch, we could all have lived in the trunk. Maybe even installed a hot tub, too.

Jeremy, in high school at the time, started calling that Buick "The Nimitz," after the aircraft carrier. We still remember The Nimitz with a certain fondness, but what do you name a coat?

To my relief (and probably everyone else's who has to look at it), my coat is starting to wear out. I lost a button, which I do plan to replace but haven't yet because I broke my thumb (don't ask) and can't steer a needle too well yet. The cuffs are starting to fray, and it's getting shiny in strategic places.

Still, there are months and months to go until spring. Maybe I'll start a support group. Surely I'm not the only woman in town who hates her coat. I'd offer to trade my dog of a coat to someone, but I'm too nice even to suggest that.

Something has to happen between now and May, though, because I'm starting to really envy the German army of World War II.

No irate letters, please; hear me out. I know Nazis were dirtbags. We historians have a tendency to play both sides of the historical line, and maybe see things differently. I always distinguish between Nazis and members of the Wehrmacht, the Germany army.

Maybe this is my guiltiest secret of all, but I've long been an admirer of those sexy, ankle-length overcoats German army officers wore. No army looked better than the German army in wintertime with those overcoats and tall boots. It was Wehrmacht *haute couture*: warm coats, well-cut coats, stylish, grey double-breasted coats with shiny buttons.

A few years ago at VCSU, I taught a class in modern European history. We spent class time watching old World War II newsreels, and I did a lot of reading. I still do, and I always end up at Stalingrad, a frightful slugfest on the Eastern Front that was the turning point of the war in Europe.

Of his namesake city, Stalin declared the Germans would not move beyond it. On the other side, Hitler said the Germans would never retreat. Between August 1942 and February 1943, two huge armies struggled by that bend in the Volga River, literally fighting room to room in the factories.

When it ended, the Wehrmacht's entire Sixth Army, bled white and starving, surrendered to victorious Soviets who marched the 600,000 survivors to prison camp. Years passed; fewer than 30,000 of those soldiers ever returned to Germany.

There is a terrible newsreel of a German POW walking by himself to internment and probable death. His beautiful grey overcoat is in shreds and he is wearing boxes on his bare feet because he has no shoes.

Suddenly, that coat I hate so well doesn't look too bad.

MAY 31, 2007

LE CRIQUET

Sorry to boast, but thanks to Jeremy, my European traveler, I now own the coolest keychain.

The French call it "le criquet," the cricket. Yep, that cricket. Jeremy also got me a 1919 French coin, but I'm betting he knows which gift made my eyes light up. I always wanted a cricket.

Here it is, almost the 63rd anniversary of the Allied invasion of Fortress Europa. Many of the old warriors are gone, so the rest of us had better keep retelling the stories.

The flights of paratroopers and lesser-known glider planes beyond the beaches of Normandy in the dark hours of June 5 and 6 were top secret in an already top secret invasion. Paratroopers and infantry on glider planes were to drop behind enemy lines to secure strategic roads and bridges in advance of the invasion.

By the nature of parachute landings, the men would be scattered over a wide area. The trick was finding each other in darkness, and for heaven's sake, doing it quietly.

How? During preinvasion days in England, someone had the bright idea to use toy tin crickets as signaling devices. A paratrooper would give one click and listen. A two-click reply meant another paratrooper was nearby.

What did it feel like to jump into German-held France in the dark? Private Leonard Griffing, 501st Parachute Infantry Regiment, US 101st Airborne Division, wrote:

"I looked at my watch. It was 12:30. When I got into the doorway, I looked out into what looked like a solid wall of tracer bullets. I said to myself, 'Len, you're in as much trouble now as you're ever going to be in. If you get out of this, nobody can ever do anything to you that you ever have to worry about.'"

If that wasn't scary enough, what about the guys on glider planes? Called "flying coffins," the wood and canvas gliders carried between 13 and 28 men into combat silently. The obvious advantage over paratroop drops was the men all landed at the same time, and didn't get scattered.

I have in my possession a photocopy of a letter written to Jim Sample, son of Bob Sample, a copilot on one of those British-made Horsa gliders that took the one-way trip into Normandy. Bob was a cousin of Jean Dugat, my high school journalism teacher. Miss D knew of my interest in military history and gave me a copy.

This was written by Edwin Rood, captain of the glider, who lost his memory of D-Day because of injuries suffered in the glider's crash landing. He pieced together this account, and his widow later sent a copy to Jim Sample, Bob's son. Here's part of it:

"We [Bob and Ed] took turns flying the glider. When we approached the landing zone . . . I took the controls, released the tow rope from the glider and started my descent to land when we were fired on by machine guns, etc.

"One machine gun bullet went through my left ankle and another penetrated the compressed air tank in our glider which provided power to operate flaps and brakes. Without flaps I could not lose altitude fast enough to hit the landing zone.

"By the same token, I was too low to clear the hedgerow into the next field. Consequently, the Horsa Glider crashed through the top of the hedge and angled nose down toward the ground. . . . My seat belt broke and I was thrown through the nose of the glider.

"Robert D. Sample, my copilot, told me [later] that he had dragged me to a ditch and covered me as best he could then reported my location to the nearest medic he could find. Then he had to leave and join the others."

Ed and Bob both survived the war. Bob was one tough hombre. From Laredo, Texas, he was one of the USDA's legendary "river riders," who patrolled the Rio Grande from Del Rio to the Gulf of Mexico, keeping out stray Mexican livestock carrying tick fever.

Bob may have survived D-Day, but he didn't survive the river. In 1982, while on river patrol, he was shot dead by someone with a grudge against the riders. His killer was never found.

I think of Bob Sample every D-Day. Now that I have my own cricket, I'll give him two clicks on June 6. Thanks, Bob and Ed, and all you thousands and thousands who gave so much.

JUNE 12, 2007

FOR THOSE IN PERIL

We interrupt this column with a news flash: Thank you, Valley City voters for supporting that ½ mil for county museums. I am so grateful. We return you to your regularly scheduled column.

I had a jolt when I read about the deadly plane crash in Ohio last weekend. Gene Damschroder, 86, farmer and former state legislator, had flown to a charity fly-in breakfast in Fremont, Ohio. He invited people to come fly with him, and five did. Gene had done this many, many times. No one knows yet what caused the crash.

I knew Gene. He and his wife, Lulu, and my folks had become friends in Florida at the end of World War II, when both men were still in the Navy. Dad stayed in the Navy, but Gene returned to Ohio, where he farmed, flew, built an airport, and spent years in the state legislature.

Dad was on duty somewhere one summer when Mom took us girls to visit the Damschroders. They had a beautiful farm and five kids, so we had fun. After dinner, Gene took us up in his small plane. It was my first ride in a plane of that size, and I was delighted with the view. Ohio in summer is a treat and a treasure, with all the green, plus the checkerboard-y fields of mostly corn.

I'm sorry Gene is gone, and sorry five others died with him, but I can't help thinking he probably died the way pilots prefer. I'm certain he wishes he had been alone in the plane, but life is strange and we really aren't in charge. Anyone who thinks otherwise just hasn't lived long enough yet.

North Dakota lost a warrior last week, too. Edward Jordan "Bud" Hagan, MD, passed away in Williston. Bud would have been 92 in October. I met him when I worked at Fort Union Trading Post National Historic Site, where he helped me with a Civil War history paper I was writing that involved a medical event.

Bud's father had been a horse and buggy doc in Williston. From an early age, Bud had gone along on some of those house calls. He decided early to be a physician, too, even though his father died when Bud was only 11.

Bud went to the University of North Dakota, took what medical courses were available then, and transferred to a medical school in Chicago to finish. He was commissioned in the US Navy even before he received his medical degree, because World War II was on and his skills were needed, literally the minute he graduated. As a naval officer, Bud chose to serve with the storied First Marine Division in the South Pacific.

Bud's war wasn't a cushy one, not with the Marines who island-hopped through the south and central Pacific, fighting a tenacious foe from the empire of Japan. He participated in landings on Cape Gloucester, Peleliu, and then Okinawa, earning a Silver Star along the way, and a couple of bronze stars for heroism in the line of duty.

I wrote Bud's story of his war, which was fascinating and full of details not commonly heard, because not that many World War II physicians ever took the time to write their battle stories. What I remember most vividly are two of his comments. "When the war ended, I looked around, and most of my friends were dead," was one. The other says a lot about physicians. In 1999, he told me that not a day went by, even then, when he did not wonder if there wasn't something more he could have done for the thousands of Marines who passed through his forward aid stations. Not a day.

Here's to both warriors, Gene and Bud. All of us Navy brats are familiar with "The Navy Hymn." It used to be sung—maybe still is—at the conclusion of Sunday services on Navy bases and is heard often at funerals.

"Eternal Father, strong to save, whose arm hath bound the restless wave. Who bids the mighty ocean deep, its own appointed limits keep. Oh, hear us, when we cry to thee, for those in peril on the sea!"

"Lord guard and guide the men who fly, through the great spaces in the sky. Be with them always in the air, in darkening storm or sunlight fair. Oh, hear us, when we lift our prayer, to those in peril in the air!"

Thank you, Gene and Bud, and good night.

PLACES AND MOVING

JANUARY 27, 2005

"YOU RANG?"

During our recent cold snap (you know, the one between mid-August and Memorial Day), I stopped at the post office. No one was at the window, but on display was what I call a hotel front-desk bell. I gave it a smart slap, it clanged, and one of the postal ladies came out quickly.

"You rang?" she joked.

I did my best British accent. "Ah, James, some stamps, if you please."

We laughed together. I bought 15 of those gorgeous cloud stamps and went on my way quite happily, even though it was ninety degrees below zero.

I dare any big city post office to match the cheer and efficiency of small town post offices, ours in particular. If you're feeling grumpy, just spend a minute at the Valley City post office and savor the warmth and good feeling of folks who care about their customers. Maybe you can judge the mood of a town by its post office. If the staff is genuinely interested in *you*, then this is a good place to buy real estate.

A few years ago, I started sending cookies to a friend who works in the National Archives in Washington, DC. He likes my oatmeal cookies, so when he does some research for me, I send him a batch.

When I mailed that first batch, I told the window lady (she retired last summer) that this was how I "paid" for research. Ever after when I mailed a cookie-sized box to Maryland, she would invariably note that the DC archivist was about to get really happy. If no one was behind me in line, we'd discuss my research. She even helped me with some ideas on a recent project involving early twentieth-century tuberculosis. Would this kind of attention happen in an urban post office? Don't hold your breath.

Years ago, when the earth's crust was still hot, we spent three years in New York City for my husband's graduate school. The postal workers were efficient, yes, but that efficiency came with a brusque, "hurry up and don't bother me" air. Under the callous scrutiny of those window trolls, I always felt like a perp from one of the wanted posters on the wall.

We eventually moved to Torrington, Wyoming. A few days after the move, I had to mail a package. My little children, the package, and I came to town. To my dismay, I discovered I didn't have quite enough money with me to mail it. I started to gather up kids and package to take home, when the postal worker stopped me.

"That's OK, I'll mail it," he told me. "Pay the rest the next time you're in town."

I was stunned. In my astonishment, I may have offered to give him my firstborn child. Or maybe I promised him a year's supply of home-cooked meals. After New York post offices, such kindness was truly an out-of-body experience. The funny thing? He was surprised at my surprise! I guess he just assumed that every post office in America operated like his.

I recently completed the World War II memoirs of a Williston doctor who served with the Marines in the South Pacific. It was horrible, dangerous duty, and his mom and three sisters were always desperate for letters. They lived next door to the post office, and those postal workers of an earlier generation would call them any time—day or night—when a letter from Dr. Hagan arrived, and take it to them. They understood just how *immediately* that widowed mother and her daughters needed to know that their son and brother was still alive.

But, really, it's not just the postal workers in small towns. We live on 4th Street SW beside a really short alley, where our garage is located. A recent snowplowing of 3rd and 4th Streets had our alley blocked at both ends by Arctic-looking ice fields. A phone call to Public Works was followed by the quick response, go-to plow guy. Who *was* that masked man? Can I make you some oatmeal cookies? Or better yet, can I always remember to treat you as well as you treat me?

FEBRUARY 10, 2005

DANCIN' IN DAKOTA

The legislature is in session. Since they debate weighty issues, I think I'll suggest to my representative that we have a state dance. The only problem with my state dance is its seasonal application; you almost never see it during summer. But since summer is a fleeting thing in North Dakota, I think it qualifies.

You've seen the dance, and I know you've done it. The dance is performed most commonly at the entrance to public buildings, between November and March for sure, and maybe longer: The dancer approaches the front door, pauses, and stomps three times. The dancer then goes inside the building, and on the carpet conveniently placed there, executes a series of shuffles. The extent of the shuffle is determined pretty much by the length of carpet.

Not only is this a distinct regional dance, but it also serves to get snow off one's boots. How like practical North Dakotans to do a dance that also involves snow removal! I never saw this dance in South Texas, and I'm pretty observant. Maybe it's Norwegian in origin. At any rate, the North Dakota Shuffle should become part of our state's law code. Minnesotans might also do the dance, so I think our legislature should act now. Write your representative, too, okay?

My other experience with dancing in North Dakota was not as successful as the shuffle. Honestly, I thought more years would have to pass before I saw that event as humorous in any way (mainly because it involved considerable pain), but I've seen the humor for several years now.

I've spent the last five summers as a ranger in the National Park Service, working at Fort Union Trading Post National Historic Site. It's located near Williston, quite close to Fort Buford State Historic Site. In July, the folks at Fort Buford invite the Sixth Infantry reenactors to set up camp and entertain visitors with firing demonstrations, cooking over a campfire, etc.

Sometimes there's a dance. Four years ago, I wore my 1860s dress—complete with hoops—to the dance on the parade ground. I'm used to long dresses, but this was my first set of hoops. Parade grounds are notoriously uneven, and my dress was a little too long. During a do-si-do, I tripped over my hoops, and put out my right hand to break my fall. You could hear the *crack!* all over the parade ground.

Everyone does agree that I fell quite gracefully. Even the EMT on site—I still see her every now and then—marveled at how calm I was. I had been dancing with Randy Kane, chief ranger at Fort Union, my boss, and also a valued friend of 31 years. A practical man, he took one look at the situation and ran for his car, which he drove onto the parade ground. In minutes, we were en route to Williston and the emergency room.

The pain was monumental. I'm not sure if feeling the bones grind together was worse that listening to them, but you get the picture. We arrived at the hospital a half hour later and went immediately to the ER.

And there we sat for several hours. Turns out there was a much more serious accident ahead of me, and the ER is small. After a while, I began to see the humor of the situation.

Picture this. Neither of us, naturally, had taken the time to change clothes. I'm sitting in my 1860s dress complete with hoops. Randy is wearing his 1870s enlisted man's infantry uniform. I couldn't help myself. I leaned over to Randy (Ooo, ouch!) and whispered, "Don't you imagine that people in here are thinking, 'Boy, you sure have to wait a long time in this emergency room!'"

He laughed, and I did that kind of hiss-laugh you do when it hurts too much to manage more. A wise woman once said (actually it was Marie Osmond, and I saw it on a calendar): "If you're going to laugh about something in five years, you might as well laugh about it right now."

I haven't worn those hoops since, although I do continue to dress in 1880s-style clothing, which isn't so hazardous. I just don't trust Yankee parade grounds.

FEBRUARY 17, 2005

WHISTLING DIXIE

February is National African-American History Month, so Georgia's on my mind.

In December 2002, our son Jeremy flew me to Charleston, South Carolina, to watch him graduate from the Border Patrol Academy. I was happy to honor him because it had been a hard slog: four months of intensive physical training, law enforcement, Spanish, and border and immigration law.

The graduation was on a Thursday. Before sunrise, the classes assembled—some 700 students—with the graduating class first. The class sizes gave evidence of the degree of program difficulty: the newest classes had complements of 50; the graduating class had 29. Fifty-percent attrition was average.

That afternoon, the government flew its newest agents out of Charleston. I took Jeremy to the airport with his shiny new badge and gun, and put him on a plane to Texas. My flight didn't leave Charleston until Sunday, so I had some time to kill. I knew I could easily kill it in Charleston, a charming Southern city, but this was a personal no-brainer. Friday morning I headed to St. Simons Island, Georgia. This woman was goin' south, headin' home.

We moved to Georgia in 1956, when my dad, a naval officer, was transferred to NAS Brunswick. St. Simons Island was nearby on one of Georgia's lovely Sea Islands. For two-plus years it was home to me, and I had never been back. After a stop further south in St. Augustine, Florida (Historians do that. I had some quickie research to do at Castillo de San Marcos National Monument), I spent Friday night on St. Simons Island.

The island had changed in 46 years from a sleepy resort with modest homes, to a trophy-house playground for the wealthy. One of the locals told me—with some regret, I think—that St. Simons Island now had the greatest per capita wealth of any place in Georgia. In essentials, though, it was much the same: the beaches as beautiful as ever, the live oak as mossy and memorable.

One thing was gone, and thank goodness. No more drinking fountains labeled "White" and "Colored." It was on St. Simons Island, Georgia, where I learned two valuable lessons: racism stinks, and my mother was a brave lady.

We rented a house that I managed to locate again on my 2002 trip. It took me back 46 years. One week back then, we needed some plumbing done that involved digging in the backyard. Two men showed up: one white, one black. The white guy got things going, and then he left. For several days, the African-American dug and fixed the pipes.

I went out to watch, and we got to talking. I was ten then, and I asked him if he was the plumber. I never forgot his answer: "Honey," he told me, "I'll never be a plumber in the state of Georgia."

That puzzled me. He was obviously doing all the work. Then it dawned on me: He was black man and could rise no higher than plumber's helper in 1956, segregated Georgia. I told him that didn't sound too fair; he just smiled and kept digging. When you're young, you care about fair, and it bothered me. And while we were on the subject, where did his kids go to school on the island? I knew it wasn't with me at my elementary school, but I was too embarrassed by then to ask.

Which brings me to my mother, the brave lady. She went to her first and only PTA meeting in Georgia one night and came home furious. With disbelief in her voice, she told us that to start the meeting, everyone sang "Dixie." "And they all stood up!" she exclaimed. I don't think I had ever seen her so angry.

"Did you stand up, Mom?" I teased.

"I. Did. Not!" she declared. Each word sounded like a whip cracking.

We kids laughed about it, and life went on, but I think about that occasionally. Here were those sons and daughters of Dixie, standing to sing that song, and there was my Idaho-raised, Yankee mom with the courage to remain seated, even though she was the only person in the room not on her feet.

Thanks, Mom.

SEPTEMBER 29, 2005

DEEP IN THE CHICKEN-FRIED HEART OF TEXAS

There are certain rules of life: Never drink orange juice after milk. No white shoes after Labor Day.

There's a third one: Only eat chicken-fried steak in Texas.

Trust me. I only eat it in Texas; no exceptions. The best one I ever ate was at the Fort Griffin General Merchandise Restaurant in Albany, a small town by Abilene.

It's run by Ali and Nariman Esfandiary, two Iranian brothers of impressive pedigree who ended up stuck in Texas after their uncle, the Shah of Iran, was deposed by the late Ayatollah Khomeini in 1979.

How people end up in places interests me, perhaps since I have traveled a lot and still marvel I am in North Dakota and like it so well.

The Esfandiarys' story began with their parents. I know this story because our son Sam is the Sysco district rep who sells the brothers their steaks and other restaurant food. We stopped at the restaurant two years ago with Sam. It was my chance for that chicken-fried steak before we left the state. Words fail me.

As we were finishing, Ali came out of the kitchen and sat down. He's in his mid-fifties, a handsome man with a moustache and those crinkly wrinkles around the eyes that most West Texans have. Sam must have told him earlier we were interested in people, because Ali started talking about his parents.

The story began in Poland before World War II. Ali and Nariman's British mother (a nurse) and her brother (a civil engineer) somehow ended up there when Germany invaded Poland in 1939. They were stuck, and found themselves "guests" of the Nazis in a detainee camp.

In 1945, either right before the war ended or right after, the brother and sister escaped, walking—you read that right—all the way to Persia (today's Iran). They arrived in Teheran and somehow met Mohammad Reza Shah Pahlavi, who had been on the Persian throne since 1941. The head of his household cavalry was a dashing officer named Jamshed Esfandiary.

The two Brits who had fled Poland ended up working in the Shah's palace. Jamshed met the English nurse; they fell in love and were married. Jamshed's sister, Soraya, became the Shah's second wife in 1953. Although the Shah divorced Soraya in 1958 when she was unable to give him an heir, the families remained close.

They lived a privileged life. Uncle Reza was a progressive monarch; he wanted his nephews educated in the United States. Ali went first. Both young men were in the US when their uncle was deposed, and the royal family and relatives fled to Egypt.

As their mother had been stuck in Poland once, they were now stuck in Texas. Ali enlisted in the Air Force. He married Patty from Iowa, and eventually became a chef at a posh country club in Abilene. Nariman joined him. They decided to take over that Fort Griffin restaurant and went to a local bank for a loan.

The banker had one question: "Do you'all fix a good chicken-fried steak?"

Ali said they did. They got the loan.

They hadn't a clue what chicken-fried steak was. They found a little old lady in Albany who taught them how to cook it. Today, the Fort Griffin General Merchandise Restaurant is renowned in the Lone Star State. In 1997, *Texas Monthly* put it on the magazine's "Top Ten Steakhouses" list, no slight honor in Texas. Tommy Lee Jones stops by whenever he can, and so does Robert Duvall. People drive long distances to eat at the Fort Griffin General Merchandise Restaurant. We drove almost three hours for the privilege.

So here's Ali, a British-Iranian American whose journey started in Poland before he was even born. He's not living a life of pampered luxury, but he's highly successful in the country he got stuck in. A writer of fiction couldn't have concocted a tale more far-fetched than this one.

Give me a chicken-fried steak cooked by the Esfandiary brothers, two West Texans who really have the knack. Ali says he'd like to go home someday and visit the Caspian Sea again. I suppose the citizens of Albany would allow that, as long as they had a guarantee he would return. In Texas, chicken-fried steak is a serious business.

OCTOBER 13, 2005

BUILDING ROADS TO SOMEWHERE

Maybe it's the gossip in me, but I like reading the newspaper's police blotter. One of my favorite items came from a few years ago, when Dacotah Bank was called Farmers and Merchants Bank. Apparently someone spotted a chicken in the parking lot, and the police impounded it. I wonder, did the chicken go peacefully? Can you fingerprint a chicken? Inquiring minds want to know.

One item a few days ago from the Valley City Police Department got me thinking: "Thursday, September 22, there was a report of a car weaving through construction on 5th Avenue; nothing was found."

I laughed. This summer past, we've all been weaving through construction in Valley City. It reminded me of Agatha Christie's book *Murder on the Orient Express*, where all the suspects were guilty of the same murder. I guess the cops had better just cuff the whole town; we all did it.

On the way to Jamestown recently, I noticed a motorist had mowed down a whole row of those skinny orange-and-white construction poles on I-94. Maybe some Valley City resident finally snapped at one too many orange-and-white poles and took it out on the Interstate. Take that! And that!

All this road construction reminded me of building the interstate system and some mega delays in the mid-'50s. I was a kid then, and it didn't register as an inconvenience. Kids don't care if they're late to things. Low on gas? Big deal; Dad will always find a filling station. Is it hot in the backseat? It doesn't matter; children assume that weather is weather. They don't discuss it because they know there's nothing they can do about it.

In the early '50s when we went vacationing to Wyoming, I remember lots of delays on two-lane highways in that state. Construction workers were blasting out mountainsides to create the interstate's four-lane highways.

Those weren't slow-down-a-little-for-ten-miles (if you feel like it) events. We came to full stops, with maybe an hour's wait, if we were lucky. Mom usually had a thermos of cold water, which always tasted like cork from the stopper.

No one had cell phones, so no one dialed and yakked. No one had laptops, so our folks couldn't catch up on office work. Blackberries were something you picked. iPods? Fuggedaboutit. Remember silence? It's nice.

What we mostly did was get out of the car, stretch, and start talking to the other waiting drivers and their carloads of kids. We got to know other Americans on the road.

I remember one family from Illinois—flatlanders—who were terrified of Wyoming's mountain roads. That struck me as strange, but the more I listened to other accents and different ideas, the more I learned about America.

Those stops were fun. When the interstates were growing, a lot of Americans got to know a lot of other Americans at the traffic delays. Some of us got to know America, too. Maybe my love of history got started during those roadside waits. I remember seeing tumbledown log cabins and wondering about the people who had lived in them.

Maybe the people who built them had been flatlanders from Illinois, new to Wyoming territory and afraid of winding roads. Now their Wyoming descendants probably never give those same roads a second thought.

Back then, we could also count on delays caused by cowboys moving cattle. Seems like our country's past was barely past during those early interstate days.

When my folks downsized their possessions and moved into assisted living last year, I requested and received a wonderful photograph, taken in the late '40s, of just such a cattle drive.

The photo was taken in Wyoming's Sunlight Basin, not far from Cody, Wyoming. The cowboys were from the Taggart family's Two-Dot Ranch. Herefords are ambling down the road in orderly fashion for a good half mile.

It's a big picture. I love to look at it and think of slower times, blasting delays, kids from all over America I would never see again, and silence interrupted by drivers taking time to meet and greet.

In the distance, we could hear progress as mountains were blasted to bits. Too bad we can't put things back the way they were. We've lost something, and I miss it.

JANUARY 5, 2006

TEN-CENT BREAD

I recently read an article about a group of people receiving their American citizenship. They had come to North Dakota from everywhere, and everyone had a story.

I have one, too, about Paul. I met him in 1975, when I was a ranger at Fort Laramie National Historic Site. That summer I worked the late shift. This particular late-summer day, the fort was just about deserted by 6:00 p.m.

Typically, when I was stationed at the captain's duplex, I dressed in 1876 clothing and sat on the porch to greet visitors. I had a view of the parade ground from my porch; I watched Paul stop at the various buildings before he came to my spot.

He was an older gentleman then; I doubt he's alive now. When he got to my porch, he sat down by me on the steps. I had noticed a lot of people liked to sit there, rest a moment, and talk. He introduced himself, but I can't recall his last name. Paul was originally from France, and he still had a slight accent, even after what must have been seventy years.

He was a visitor, so I told him about the captain's duplex and a little of the history of what was happening at Fort Laramie in 1876. (Quite a lot; this was the summer Custer bought the farm in Montana, and Fort Laramie was a staging area for one of the prongs of that campaign.)

I invited Paul to go inside and look around. He did, then came back to my porch to sit some more. As I said, he was old, and it was a long walk around the parade ground.

I asked him to tell me something about himself, and he obliged. His wife of many years had died the year before, and he decided to drive around the country. He lived in California's Bay Area.

Then he told me how he came to America. His father and uncle were coal miners in the rich mines in northern France that had changed hands frequently with Germany, depending on the fortunes of war. Right around the turn of the century, there was a disastrous cave-in.

Both men survived the calamity, but when Paul's father was pulled from the rubble, he and his brother decided that was the end. They were going to America.

Both men had wives and young children. They sold everything and arranged passage to America in steerage class. No steward put chocolates on the pillows in steerage, but I'm betting most of our ancestors came that way.

The brothers had an uncle in Oakland, California. He had sent his address and offered to help them get started in America. When the two families reached New York City, and passed successfully through the health inspection at Ellis Island, they took the train west.

Paul had a smile on his face when he told me the story. "They couldn't speak any English," he said, "except for one phrase: 'ten-cent bread.'"

They had learned that a loaf of bread in America cost a dime. They still had some cheese and sausage brought from France and enough money to make it to California if they augmented that with ten-cent bread.

Every time the train stopped, the brother would leap off, find the nearest bakery, and tell the baker, "Ten-cent bread, *s'il vous plait*."

"They didn't know how to ask for five loaves of bread, so they'd take the bread, bow, pay the dime, and then say, 'Ten-cent bread,' over and over until they had enough," Paul said. "They did that all across the country."

The families arrived in San Francisco late at night, tired, travel-worn, and without enough English to locate their uncle. "My father found a policeman and showed him the address in Oakland," Paul told me.

There wasn't any Oakland Bay Bridge then, but only a ferry to cross the bay. Somehow, the policeman made them understand that he wanted them to wait right there. His shift was about over, and he wasn't going to leave them stranded.

When Paul told me the story, he still had wonder in his voice. "He took us on that ferry all the way across the bay, right to my uncle's door, then tipped his hat and said good night."

Welcome to America, land of ten-cent bread and big-hearted cops.

JANUARY 26, 2006

"A MIGHTY WOMAN WITH A TORCH"

I've never hung out in diplomatic circles, but for a while in Brooklyn, New York, we lived in the Albanian Embassy.

That's what we called the four-story walk-up on 18th Avenue, where we lived from 1969 to 1972 while Martin studied for his master of fine arts in directing from Brooklyn College.

We lived on the second floor in a building that had seen better days. If I recall right, the foyer had a marble floor. By 1969, the superintendent of the building (called a super) just skimmed a dirty mop over that floor if he felt like it and called it good.

It wasn't much of a building, but it became a history lesson to me. After a year there, I realized I could trace the social history of the United States by our building's supers. It was a case study of what happens in an upwardly mobile society, such as we enjoy here in America.

When we moved in, the super and his family were African-American. Supers were paid what couldn't have been much of a salary, but were furnished with living space. In exchange for this largess, the super's job was to keep things running and make minor repairs when tenants had complaints.

I figured a super was a "starter" job, employment you get when you breeze into town with no skills. Entry level. First stop on the way to the American Dream.

After a few months, the super moved on and the managing company hired a Puerto Rican. His English wasn't too good, but we all managed. I figured the African-American super had found a better job, and moved himself and his family off that bottom rung. You know: today, a super; tomorrow, the world on a cracker.

A year later, the Puerto Ricans left—again, probably to a better job—and the Albanians came. I don't know how many families there actually were; two at least, crammed into one flat probably no bigger than our apartment directly above them.

The women all wore headscarves, which mystified me at the time. Now I suppose they probably were Muslims. No one seemed to speak any English at all, which made it problematic when the rest of us in the building needed something fixed.

This was years before the breakup of the Soviet Union and its subsidiary Balkan States. I wondered how on earth they had managed to get to the United States, but had no common language with them to find out. They remained a mystery.

I didn't know anything about them, except they were following the building's social history pattern, and now stood on the lowest job rung in New York City (or so I imagined).

Other Albanian families moved in, so we started calling our building the Albanian Embassy. When spring came, the Albanian women opened their windows and hollered to each other across the courtyard in their exotic language. We dubbed one of them "Souvlaki."

The kitchen smells bubbling up from the Albanian super's apartment below us were not tantalizing. I don't know what they ate, but it smelled worse than haggis.

Then it was finally our turn to leave the Albanian Embassy. Martin got his MFA. We were upwardly mobile now, and on to a job at a community college in Torrington, Wyoming. We bid a fond farewell to the embassy, but I have wondered since then: Who replaced the Albanians?

It may have been Haitians. They were coming into the country in greater numbers by 1972. It may have been Laotians, or maybe Cambodians, then Estonians, or Latvians, then maybe Sudanese.

It's been more than 30 years. The Albanians probably have college graduates among their children and grandchildren by now. Ditto the Haitians and Laotians that I imagine came later. Guess what? We were all upwardly mobile in the Albanian Embassy.

I think of the Statue of Liberty, and those words about "your tired, your poor, your huddled masses yearning to breathe free" that have become almost trite and hackneyed to some.

Not to me. I remember the Albanian Embassy and wish its strange and exotic employees well. They're probably citizens now, living somewhere in this land where there is room enough for all.

The Lady in the Harbor still lifts her "lamp beside the golden door." Wherever you are, Souvlaki, do you still see it?

JUNE 8, 2006

VOTING FOR THE CROOK

Sometimes events coincide with words not ordinarily seen as associated with each other. That happened to me a month ago when I saw the following headline online: "Xiang Xiang released into the wild."

This happened to be around the same time the president of the People's Republic of China was visiting the United States. When I saw the Xiang Xiang headline, my mind had an instant picture of the president being thrust out of a cage and (what else?) released into the wild, hiding behind bamboo shoots and swimming polluted rivers.

No, wait. The president of China is Hu Jin Tao; Xiang Xiang is the first panda born and raised in captivity to be released into a Chinese forest. Silly me.

It got me thinking, though, about people I'd like to see released into the wild and forced to survive on roots and berries and the occasional Pringle thrown from a passing car.

Politicians come first. We lived in Monroe, Louisiana, for five years, which took us through one governor's election cycle. This was when David Duke, white supremacist and former grand wizard of the goons in sheets, decided he'd like to be governor of Louisiana. Really bad idea. The state had enough troubles, even back then, without adding Duke to the list. Even Louisianans joke about having the best food and the worst politicians.

Through a bit of slick political maneuvering (Louisiana may have cornered the market on slick political tricks), Duke defeated a far more palatable opponent in the primaries, which left many of us wondering, "Huh?"

There he was, set to run against former governor Edwin Edwards, a Cajun even slicker than Duke. Everyone knew Edwards was a crook, but there's a lot of nudge-nudge wink-wink in Louisiana politics. Maybe that's changed now. And maybe I'm going to sprout wings and call myself a Cessna.

Both candidates reeked. What's a voter to do? All of a sudden, it became absolutely necessary that Duke was defeated, even if it meant giving Edwards another chance to dip his fingers in the gumbo and pull out corruption by the yard.

Cars started wearing the most amazing bumper sticker: "Vote for the crook. It matters." I can't even fathom such a sign in North Dakota, where governors (recent ones, anyway) are bland, honest, competent, and probably even buy their own groceries and stand in post office lines.

So we voted for the crook, because it did matter, and the crook was elected. I was happy, but it was an odd feeling to stand in a voting booth and pull the lever for Edwards, someone I'd probably avoid if I saw him on the street.

Edwards did get released into the wild after his term. The feds nabbed him on a racketeering charge and he's in the slammer until 2011. Last I heard of Duke, he'd gotten an honorary degree from a racist university in the Ukraine. They can keep him.

It wasn't so hard to vote for Edwards. I taught an early-morning religion class for high school kids in our church. One of my students was a little charmer named Tisha, whose African-American parents were a pharmacist and a nurse and who lived down the street from us.

It was safe to say Tisha lived a sheltered life, protected and secure in her friendships and family. We still hear from Tisha and her folks occasionally; I know we'll probably see them again.

We were discussing that gubernatorial election and David Duke one morning in class, and the subject of the Ku Klux Klan came up. I've never seen such terror on one person's face as on Tisha's. We thought she was joking at first, but it soon became painfully obvious she wasn't. She was truly frightened of the idea of David Duke governing her lovely state.

I'm sure she had no experience with night riders or lynch mobs—that was an earlier time—but stories like that go deep into a people's psyche.

As disturbed as I was about voting for Edwards, all I had to do was think about Tisha and pull that lever for her. Easiest thing I ever did.

I like to think I learned one thing from that Louisiana election: Be really careful who you vote into public office.

June 15, 2006

THANK YOU FOR FLYING AIR PRIBILOF

My daughter Liz and I are a disgrace to Deep Thinkers. While driving home from seeing *X-Men: The Last Stand* instead of discussing serious stuff, we debated what mutant powers we want.

Liz wants to be a teleporting mutant. She doesn't own a car right now, and walks to work. This mutation would simplify her life. She also wants to be a mutant who can find anything, anywhere.

Moms already possess that gene. It is activated when the doc smacks her firstborn on the rump. After my son was born, if the doctor had suddenly misplaced the afterbirth, I could have told him right where it was.

Moms, you know this gene. When a kid hollers she can't find one shoe, you can tell her it's under her bed in the left back quadrant, right next to missing puzzle pieces and Jimmy Hoffa.

Liz also wants to be a perfect-grammar mutant, whose power is to blast those afflicted with the "where's it at" curse into a thousand tiny pronouns.

I had to disagree. This mutation only matters to people already living on Planet Grammaria. The others wouldn't know *lie* from *lay* if it bit them on the gerund.

Let me be a flying mutant, now that airlines are charging extra for everything except airsick bags. Pretty soon, travelers will have to provide their own pilots. We already use ticketless tickets; maybe flightless flights are next.

Some airlines are charging for extra bags, which means people will probably start wearing clothes over their clothes. You'll recognize them. They'll look like the Von Trapp family escaping over the Alps, wearing four pair of lederhosen, six headscarves, and three pairs of shoes each.

I won't miss airline food. We who fly steerage have noticed a decline since the glory days of stale peanuts. It's easy to just say no to Styrofoam pretzels, so what's to miss?

I prefer to carry my own food, anyway. I hope airlines will draw the line at fellow travelers grilling in the aisle or stomping their own grapes. If you must eat liverwurst, kindly don't breathe between takeoff and "buh-bye."

Maybe I already have the teleporting gene. Years ago, I flew from Seattle to Anchorage and arrived there before I departed, thanks to time changes. How cool is that?

What a trip. In Anchorage, I switched to the legendary Reeve Aleutian Airways (Alaska's first airline) for my daylong flight to Adak Island. It's in the middle of the Aleutian Island chain, and my dad was stationed there.

Those pilots were already mutants because they could fly anywhere, in (almost) any weather. The Aleutians are notorious as the home of all weather. In the summer I spent on Adak, the sun shone twice.

Because it was May, and school was out, we all got a bonus: a free trip to the Pribilof Islands. Airlines today would find a way to charge us for that side trip, I am sure. Let's keep this our little secret, eh?

The Aleutian Islands are like a chain extending into the Pacific Ocean. The Pribilofs—four small islands—are at the apex of that chain. Next stop: Russia. Annually, one million fur seals return to the island to breed. It's also a birder's paradise.

Native Aleut kids who had spent the winter in mainland boarding schools were returning to the Pribilofs, which explained our side trip and scary landing. There is no flying visibility around the Bering Sea. When a descent starts, you hope there is something down there, because it's not in sight until touchdown.

The runway was gravel. We bumped to a stop, and the Aleut kids deplaned. I looked out the window onto absolute bleakness. It was raining, and the wind (it never stops blowing in the Aleutians) was blowing it sideways.

The kids met their folks, and we took off. I couldn't see a town anywhere, so I craned around for a final glimpse of St. Paul Island before it vanished in the fog.

There it was, a tiny village clinging to the rocks over a restless sea that will kill you if you fall in and remain longer than a minute. Those kids looked so happy to be home, and *that* was home?

I'm a little wiser now. Home is anywhere people love you. And I'll bet those Aleut mothers have that same mutant gene and know precisely where their children leave their mukluks and sled dogs.

SEPTEMBER 7, 2006

ACROSS THE WIDE MISSOURI

I spent Labor Day weekend as I have for the last six years: at Fort Union Trading Post National Historic Site, slaving over a cook stove and fighting a losing battle with flies.

It's part of Living History Weekend, when reenactors, rangers, and muzzleloaders dress up (or more generally down) as *engagés*, *Métis*, and Indians. Of course, some of the Indians really are Indians, so we have an air of authenticity. After three smelly days of wood smoke and sweat, we have a fragrant authenticity, too.

No one's there just for show. During the year, the guys have researched Fort Union and planned a building project for the site, something both useful and historic.

They've built sheds inside the fort against the wall, a massive fur press out front, a smaller screw press, a scaled-down mackinaw boat. Big stuff. That fur press can pack a bunch of buffalo robes into a compact bundle: 19th-century shrinkwrap.

This year the project was a corral outside the east wall for the horses and donkeys that sometimes come along.

It's a rendezvous, too. Several rangers who've worked there before return for the fun. One is now a backcountry ranger at Yellowstone National Park. Another, who used to work at Knife River NHS, is chief of interpretation at Little Bighorn Battlefield National Monument.

We women cook for the living history laborers on a stove set up behind the Bourgeois House. It's a beast, modeled on a 19th-century army cook stove, so slightly out of period for the earlier era of the fur trade.

It's dangerous around that stove and we know it. Last year one of our number was burned, so we have even more respect. No one gets near it without leather gloves. I always watch my long skirts, too, when I'm cooking. Our extreme care helps keep us safe.

Our caution reminds me of the lift bridge over the Missouri River a few miles upstream. The bridge was built in 19-early-something and designed to rise in the middle for tall-masted river traffic. The lift was only used once, I believe, but railroad tracks still cross it.

Up to 1981, that railroad bridge, the only convenient crossing for miles, was also used by cars and trucks. I kid you not. There is still planking for cars between the railroad tracks.

An insurance company investigating the situation once described it as the most dangerous bridge in America. In the next sentence, though, the writer added that because it was so dangerous, it was probably safe. People were careful about getting on that bridge, because there was simply no margin for error.

I heard all this from Bob Kisthart, that Yellowstone backcountry ranger. He and I drove out to the lift bridge once after work and walked on it. The mechanism to raise and lower the center section is long gone, part of a scrap drive during one of the world wars in the past century.

The bridge is still usable by trains and cars, but there is a standard bridge across the Missouri now. The old risk factor and racing pulse are things of the past.

I learned a lot from Bob. He's a real mountain man. He hunts with his black powder muzzleloader and makes most of his deerskin clothing and 19th-century-style shirts.

The coolest thing about Bob is his attitude. When someone gives him a challenge, rather than automatically saying, "I don't know how to do that," he studies the matter and does it. He doesn't whine or demand a feasibility study; he just does what he sets out to do. The cool thing? Because he knows he can do anything, he really *can*. He's the poster child for competency.

I watched him make a Sioux willow backrest one summer. He had a picture in a book and that was all. He went to the Missouri, got the willows, soaked them so he could shape them, then made the backrest.

My son Jeremy spent two years in Brazil once, speaking Portuguese exclusively. I think this surprised him as much as anyone, because when he was in high school, he was the French teacher's nightmare.

He learned Portuguese because he had to. When he moved to Texas, he picked up Spanish because he knew he could; no question.

The knowing is in the doing.

JANUARY 18, 2007

"ALL I ASK IS A TALL SHIP…"

I'm a telemarketer's nightmare. No one can hang up faster than I can when the phone rings and there's a telltale space before someone asks for Carla Kelly in a harried voice.

I hung up on Sam once, when he faked a Chinese accent. Wounded, he called right back in his normal voice, but he got the message: Don't mess with Mom on the telephone. She knows she didn't order egg rolls from the Mandarin Palace.

On the other hand, I'm a sucker for bath products with the words "ocean" or "sea breeze" in them.

I feed my fantasy when I'm standing by a Suave products display: inexpensive goodies for those of us of modest income.

Several months ago, missing the ocean, I bought Suave shampoo and conditioner called Ocean Breeze, even though I didn't really need it.

There I was this morning, washing my hair with Ocean Breeze and trying to remember John Masefield's poem "Sea Fever":

"I must go down to the sea again, to the lonely sea and the sky,
And all I ask is a tall ship, and a star to steer her by."

Masefield was England's poet laureate years ago, but he was no Keats or Shelley. Still, Masefield was right about the ocean being a "must" on occasion.

What a disappointment. The shampoo didn't smell anything like seaweed or saltwater. At least I had a poetic moment in the shower, which beats most mornings, when I'm thinking about stuff to write at the newspaper.

I miss the ocean. By now, I've lived more years in the center of the nation than on its fringes, but the ocean is always there, somehow.

I found one cure better than shampoo. Almost two years ago, I took the train to St. Paul, Minnesota. Bob Turner, my former brother-in-law, picked me up in a 1993 Camry I had located online in his city, and he arranged for the purchase.

Bob wanted to drive to Duluth, where his parents live, for the purpose of a test drive. His folks needed some computer assistance, so Bob thought he'd combine a shakedown cruise and the geek help.

This suited me fine, because I liked Bob. I don't think Bob and I had ever spent that many hours with just each other for company, and it turned out to be grand.

As we neared Duluth—my first visit—Bob started to prep me for the view of Lake Superior. I was ready to be mildly impressed. I'm well seasoned enough to know that too much anticipation often means disappointment.

Not this time; Lake Superior is well named. We topped that rise, and, my goodness, there was the ocean. I had no idea something so ocean-like existed so far inland. There was water as far as I could see, even if it was frozen.

I need to go back in June, when Superior is open water. For now, I'll grumble and settle for my $1.78 bottle of Ocean Breeze.

Proust got it right; smells do jog the memory. Years ago, I visited Santa Fe, that marvelous New Mexico town formally founded in 1610. For more than 400 years, actually, people have been burning aromatic, greasy, piñon pine in the low-ceilinged houses. The whole town smells of piñon pine.

Before I left Santa Fe, I bought some pressed piñon pine incense. During the summer, I'd light the incense and my kids and I would sit in the backyard and enjoy the pungent fragrance. Unlike the fake Ocean Breeze, that incense smelled exactly like Santa Fe.

Sam, a district sales manager for Sysco Corporation in West Texas, decided to change Sysco houses. He had a job interview in Taos, New Mexico, before Christmas.

He called to talk about the job and told me, "Mom, the whole area smells just like that incense you used to burn. I drove around with a smile on my face."

And I had a smile on mine, pleased to know Sam remembered.

I'm sure we'll visit him in New Mexico. Until then, I might have to ask him to find me some of that piñon pine incense.

I've been missing Liz, who lives in Midland, Texas, now. I have a recipe I call West Texas Yahoo! Pecan Bark. Maybe I'll make some. It doesn't smell like oil wells, dust storms, or javelinas, thank goodness, but the Yahoo! is there.

Travel in a whiff.

MAY 17, 2007

THE MAGIC BACKPACK

Like most kids, my son Jeremy used a backpack in high school. He was also a fan of MacGyver, that resourceful secret agent who could MacGyver his way out of dicey situations by using duct tape and a Swiss army knife.

I'm not sure how it started, years ago, but Jeremy developed the "magic backpack." Need some Swiss cheese? Poof. It's in the backpack. Can't find leather booties for your sled dogs? Check the backpack. Need a road map for Somalia? Well, you know where it is. Antibiotics for leprosy? Bingo.

Jeremy's in France now. He's been in Europe since early May, and he's living out of a backpack. On Sunday, he called from Paris to wish me happy Mother's Day. In the course of our conversation, he said that whenever he runs across Americans, they can't believe he's traveling so light.

I'm not surprised; Jeremy is MacGyver-resourceful. He's also a careful planner. He figured out this trip—from Budapest to Paris via Eastern Europe—by himself. There were certain things he wanted to see: Auschwitz; Prague; Krakow's St. Mary's Church, where the trumpeter plays the broken note; and Normandy's D-Day beaches.

He's discovered some basic truths: People speak English in Europe. He told me Sunday, "Mom, if you want to know what the world's most useful language is, we already speak it." Nice to know.

Basic Truth Two: Greece has the most beautiful women.

Three: He wrote, via e-mail, that Italy has cornered the market on pastries and gelato (ultimate ice cream). "I cannot say I have been to every bakery in Venice, but I haven't seen them all, either."

I e-mailed him to feed a pigeon in Venice's St. Mark's Square for me, and he replied: "I fed some pigeons in St. Mark's for you. I just happened to have a gelato cone in my hand. Not that I wanted a gelato, but you wanted the pigeons fed." Good son.

Before Venice, he was in Krakow, Poland, where he met two brothers from Arizona, law enforcement guys like him. The three of them rented a car and drove to Auschwitz. They also visited the salt mines, where whole churches and elaborate buildings have been carved out of salt, hundreds of feet underground.

Jeremy summed up Auschwitz this way. One of the brothers asked the other, "Would you rather be a tourist guide in the salt mines or at Auschwitz?"

The reply: "The salt mines. At least I can explain those."

When he e-mailed me that he had taken a train from Auschwitz, I e-mailed back something like: "It's must be a good feeling to say you've taken a train *from* Auschwitz, instead of *to* Auschwitz." He replied: "Yeah, believe me, the significance was not lost on me."

He went to Athens from Italy, toured the Acropolis, dodged suicidal scooters, and escaped to a Greek island in the Cyclades he couldn't pronounce. He spent a couple of days there, tried their ice cream (good, but not gelato), made his observations about the women, then flew to Paris.

He went directly from Paris to Normandy. I think the D-Day beaches are probably the reason he made the whole trip, my backpack son who loves history. I can almost see him walking Omaha, Utah, Juno, Sword, and Gold beaches, looking up at Point du Hoc, and wondering how on earth the Rangers scaled the 100-meter high cliffs without a magic backpack. But they did. I hope the day he was there was overcast and misty, and the tide high, as on June 6, 1944. I know he's looking once for himself and once for me.

Ralph Waldo Emerson called traveling a "fool's paradise." Obviously he never traveled with a magic backpack, which is located in the heart. I've traveled to Europe in my heart for years. Now that my son is there, I'm almost seeing what he's seeing.

As I'm sitting here, I got the bright idea to go on the Internet and see if I could find a site that actually plays the *hejnal* from St. Mary's Church, the one the trumpeter played in the 13th century to warn the townsfolk of the approaching Tatar army. He got an arrow in the throat for his pains. Every day since then, a trumpeter has played that *hejnal* in his honored memory. When the note breaks off, that's when he died.

I found such a site. I played it. Now that's in my magic backpack, too.

OCTOBER 4, 2007

AN OCEAN CRUISE

Our daughter Liz—some of you know her—moved to Midland, Texas, more than a year ago, and recently married Mike Elliott from Wisconsin. Liz called the other day and in the course of the conversation, mentioned how much she missed the post office here in Valley City.

I understand. Without exception, the postal workers are friendly, helpful, and pleasant to do business with. There also aren't any excruciatingly long lines of people standing there since the Spanish-American War, waiting for service.

The postal workers share their funny stories, too. Here's my current favorite. One of the window workers took a package from a woman, weighed it, and went into the spiel we all know: "Is there anything fragile, liquid, perishable, or potentially hazardous?"

The customer listened politely then replied, "No, but thank you for asking." Yep, North Dakota nice with a sense of humor.

I'm a big fan of US stamps. The latest beauty is a triangle stamp commemorating the 400th anniversary of the settlement of Jamestown in what is now Virginia. It's a great stamp, with illustrations of the *Susan Constant*, *Godspeed*, and *Discover*, the three ships that brought the first settlers to what was then a continent peopled mostly by Indians and Spaniards.

I used to live in Virginia, and I've been to Jamestown, America's first permanent English settlement. The fort is triangular, which is nicely reflected in the new stamp. (North Dakota has its own triangular fort, a reconstruction of the fort built by Lewis and Clark and the Corps of Discovery for their winter among the Mandan in 1804–1805, and named Fort Mandan.)

Jamestown was a pathetic settlement for years, plagued by violence, poor crops, disease, and dissension. Captain Christopher Newport (interesting man), who helmed the *Susan Constant*, made several voyages to and from Jamestown. John Rolfe was a passenger on one of those voyages, the survivor of a shipwreck that took the lives of his wife and child. Rolfe had tobacco seeds with him, which he planted in Virginia, and which gave the struggling colony a money crop.

Say what you will about tobacco—I'm emphatically not in favor of it—the crop allowed Virginia to survive and eventually thrive. By November 11, 1620, when the *Mayflower* made landfall at what is now Cape Cod, Massachusetts, the settlers of Jamestown and those who followed had founded several more towns in Virginia. They were the veterans of life in America, and the pilgrims the newbies.

I'm in awe of the early settlers of both Virginia and Massachusetts. It's hard to grasp either the dedication or the desperation that would send people across a stormy ocean in fall and winter to a new land. Of the 102 passengers who sailed on the *Mayflower*, about half died during that first winter of 1620–1621. Similar averages were recorded among Jamestown's first settlers. The weak just didn't make it, and there was no help for them.

Knowing a little about *Mayflower* history was a bonus this summer, when my sisters and I went to Plymouth, England. Plymouth today is a city of 240,000 people, and home to one of the UK's two major naval bases. The city was bombed extensively by the Luftwaffe during World War II, with most of the damage to the city center. The strategic dockyards were hit, but not as badly as the center, which has been rebuilt.

The Barbican, the oldest part of town along the docks, is still there, and charming, with narrow streets, claustrophobic alleys, and buildings that were old when the pilgrims left on September 6, 1620. One building on the waterfront lists all the *Mayflower's* passengers on an exterior wall.

The Mayflower Steps are justly famous. They lead right down to the water and were supposedly used by the pilgrims as they boarded their ship. Some say the real steps are now under the Admiral MacBride, a pub built at water's edge in the late 18th century.

I don't know the truth of that, but I enjoyed walking down those steps and getting into a boat for a harbor tour. I couldn't help but wonder: Would I have been brave enough to take that passage to the New World? Hard to say, but I do know some of my ancestors made the later crossing to Massachusetts Bay Colony in the mid-17th century. Maybe they left from Plymouth, a town that has all my affection, now that I've seen it.

OCTOBER 5, 2006

BEFRIEND A NAUGA TODAY

I've been fooling a lot of folks in town. People seem to think I've done a lot of things in my life. Not so. What I do is remember the ordinary stuff that happens.

This time of year, when the air turns nippy and Honeycrisp apples are for sale, I think of my grandfather, the mighty elk hunter from Cody, Wyoming.

I was 4. We were staying in Cody because my dad was in Thailand, helping create the Thai Air Force. Grandpa had shot an elk, and the colossal animal was stretched out on the garage floor.

Grandma and I were standing there, and I told her seriously, "Now we won't starve this winter."

I was too young to remember the comment, but it's firmly fixed in family lore, so I don't doubt I said it. If I had possessed any inkling then that my interests would point me to Western American history, I should have said, "Now there will be meat in the lodge."

There's probably not a college student alive who doesn't remember "mystery meat," that curious entrée that showed up with dismal regularity in the cafeteria. I opted for salads on mystery meat night.

I don't search for causes, but sometimes they find me. I am referring to the Nauga. Sometime during the '70s, the Nauga crawled out of the Everglades, or possibly emerged from the blank space on the map that Rand-McNally called North Dakota.

(No, Mr. Rand and Mr. McNally, I have not forgotten that year you two neglected to put North Dakota in your atlas. Even we transplanted North Dakotans with nary an ounce of Scandinavian DNA develop long memories here. Maybe it's the endless winters or those orange-and-white construction cones that do something weird to the frontal lobe.)

Anyway, suddenly there were Nauga. To my knowledge, I've never eaten Nauga. For all I know, it tastes remarkably like chicken. Nauga fast food eateries have never sprung up; perhaps it's the source of mystery meat.

Which reminds me: I was back in Carlisle, Pennsylvania, a few years ago on business. When in Rome, I like to try local delicacies. It was breakfast; I asked the waitress about scrapple.

She looked around, leaned forward and whispered in conspiratorial tones: "Honey, you don't want to try it." Honey didn't; she's no foo'.

Ah, the Nauga. It's the hyde of the Nauga that apparently attracts the most interest with its durability and color range. Biologists don't know what causes the extreme color variations. Perhaps male Nauga brighten up during the mating season to attract the more drab brown female Nauga.

The hyde is indestructible. There was a time when coats were made of the Nauga's hyde. Trouble is, the stuff never wears out. When mankind tired of Nauga coats, they ended up stuffed in closets beside polyester suits and Nehru jackets.

Seeking for useful information about Nauga (I do this so you won't have to), I turned to Wikipedia, that Internet site which is the sole source used in most college research papers.

The mystery is solved. Apparently the Nauga is a shy water creature found in the Naugatuck River in Connecticut.

Nauga hunters work at night, shining their flashlights on the river. Ever curious, male Nauga surface and are easy pickings for hunters. The creatures are then sorted by color.

It's a tough world for Naugas. They suffer indignities like the disdain heaped on orange and earth tone couches—also from the '70s—that outlived their popularity. In years past, the Inuit abandoned their old folks on ice floes. It's not so easy to dispose of those orange-and-brown sofas.

Sometimes you'll find one tucked in disgrace in a corner somewhere, sulking, its self-esteem in shreds. Approach it quietly, averting your gaze, holding out your hand so it can sniff you. Talk softly.

One of these sad creatures skulks by the elevator on the first floor in McCarthy Hall at VCSU. The rejection must be enormous.

This just in: I sent my son Jeremy a copy of this column last week, and he e-mailed me: "Frankly, I was shocked that you would talk so much about Naugas and not even mention the millions of wontons slaughtered each year just for their skins, which are deliciously crunchy when deep fried."

Omigosh, I forgot the wontons. We'd better start a taskforce.

JUNE 19, 2007

BLOOD AND RAIN

Maybe it did rain on our parade a bit last week, but what landed on us, courtesy of Mother Nature, was a wake-up call that we don't control the elements. Although we weren't devastated like Cedar Falls, Iowa, folks who remember Grand Forks in 1997 probably had a painful reminder.

I'm humbled by how often destruction brings out the best in people. After a disaster, for every gouger who raises the price of generators or Grinch who loots a neighbor, there are more kind hearts who help.

Did any of you see the 1984 motion picture *Starman*? Jeff Bridges played an alien on the run from the usual movie assortment of government stereotypes. Toward the end, when things are tough, the alien makes this profound observation about us earthlings: "When things are at their worst, you people are at your best."

The center of the nation has seen a lot of that "worst" in the past few weeks. Tornados are a way of life here. North Dakota has received its share of hammering in recent years; in recent weeks, so have Minnesota and Wisconsin. Kansas, Nebraska, and Iowa have been pounded by twisters, plus floodwaters are high in some areas.

Through it all, we've witnessed heroism, no more so than at the Little Sioux Scout Ranch in the Loess Hills of western Iowa, where a tornado "went through camp like a bowling ball," in the words of Michael Chertoff, Secretary of Homeland Security. Ninety-three boys between 13 and 18 were attending a leadership training session when that tornado hit. Four Scouts were killed and many injured.

I watched a television interview with one Scout who described the dining hall where many of the boys took shelter and which collapsed around them or blew away. He said the floor was pink with blood and rain. That's not an observation you want any of your children to have to make, but there it was, ugly and raw. The young man was composed, direct, and adult in his comments. He had been through an experience most us never have to endure.

He and the other Scouts were prepared. They dug out their fellow Scouters from the rubble, applying tourniquets where needed, compression bandages, and immediate aid. They did what Scouts are taught to do. Iowa Governor Chet Culver—there's an overworked governor—said, "There were some real heroes at this Scout camp."

I doubt a single Scout in the camp felt like a hero. They told reporters they were only doing what they learned, sounding a lot like the old guys from World War II who just smile when people say they were the Greatest Generation. A tornado is a tough teacher, but there was a camp full of champion learners. I would say they all passed the requirements of any leadership session.

Aaron Eilert, Sam Thomsen, Josh Fennen, and Ben Petrzilka died when the tornado roared through camp. Their families are hurting right now in the worst way possible, because there's something so terrible about children dying. It's out of tune with how things should be, in the order of life, but tornados and high water are no respecters of persons.

In the middle of grief I can only imagine, Ben's parents have already established funds to build underground storm shelters at Little Sioux Scout Ranch. They don't want any other boys or families to go through what Ben and his friends suffered. They are channeling their grief into a noble effort that will bless others' lives.

Here in Valley City, when that storm tore through last week, folks thought of their neighbors. We had a massive limb down in our yard. That afternoon, my neighbor, BJ Edwardson, and her granddaughters, Sydney and Sam Nelson, stopped by. BJ said her granddaughters had picked up the sticks and twigs in her yard, and they wanted to do the same in mine.

The twins went right to work. I asked BJ if I could pay them for their effort, but she said no. She wanted Sydney and Sam to know the good feeling that comes from helping others. I think BJ is the best grandma on the planet. She's teaching her darlings that what's inside matters and that one of the by-products of service is character. Another is happiness.

Our thanks also to Gerri Hammond across the street. Martin was sawing that pesky limb, using only Martin-power. She handed him a chain saw.

Neighbors. That's what they do.

WRITING AND EDUCATION

MARCH 31, 2005

THE BEST TEACHER I EVER HATED

Now that I'm working for the *Times-Record*, I've been assigned Jefferson Elementary School as my beat. I see excellent teachers there who are most certainly making a difference in their students' lives. I'm reminded of Jean Dugat—Miss D—my high school journalism teacher.

I attended A. C. Jones High School in Beeville, Texas. Some of my friends worked on the *Trojan*, our school newspaper, so I gravitated in that direction after my freshman year.

I would have started sooner, except that I was afraid of Miss D, a stern mountain of a woman. She expected perfection. Demanded it.

I wanted to write, *had* to write, and finally decided to brave the dragon. No article was allowed in the *Trojan* that wasn't perfect. So what if we were just 14- through 18-year-old journalists? We had to be professional. She was deadly serious about that.

That was when I learned never to use the word *very* in a news story. If Miss D saw that word trembling on the page, out came the red pen.

Once I got over my fears, we actually got along well enough. I eventually asked her what was wrong with *very*.

"It doesn't mean anything," she told me. "You might as well write 'damn.'"

That was when I began to understand the stewardship of words. There was simply no substitute for the right word. What you committed to paper had to be the right words. It mattered.

This journalistic rigor, painful as it was, paid off. In my junior year, our little mimeographed paper won the "Tops in Texas" award the first year it was created. Mind you, our competition came from Houston and San Antonio schools—the Big Boys. We were that good.

I was named feature editor in my senior year, which suited me fine. Along with the job came the chance to drive here and there in Texas with Miss D to see professional journalism in action. She had a willing accomplice in her uncle Gentry Dugat, a cigar-chomping journalist of the old school, who finagled me a spot in the press box when President Lyndon B. Johnson spoke at a nearby university. I wrote a feature article about the experience for the *Trojan*.

My biggest story was a feature about the restoration of Presidio la Bahia, America's only complete Spanish *presidio* (fort), in nearby Goliad. I wrote, and rewrote, and rewrote. A few years earlier, I would have hated Miss D by then. All those rewrites! I didn't hate her anymore, because now I knew she was turning me into a writer.

Finally, the article came back from her desk on Mount Olympus with no red marks. We published the article in the *Trojan*—part one of a Texas Tours segment—and entered it in statewide competition against all those big schools.

It won first place. I've won writing awards since then, but none has ever meant as much to me as that feature about Presidio la Bahia. Since then, I've visited the presidio several times, because I *own* it, through countless rewrites. Don't know why they still charge me admission.

Twenty years passed. I kept writing and stayed in touch with Miss D. She called at odd times, and we chatted. I returned to Beeville for my class reunion and stayed with Miss D. We sat up way too late each night, talking.

A few years after that, she died suddenly, and I flew back for the funeral. The church was packed with former students. Rev. Janice Huie, editor the year I was feature editor, conducted the services. Miss D's pallbearers were all former students.

A few years after that, I returned to Beeville during the Easter season and stayed with another former editor, a Spanish teacher now. Kay had some *cascarones* on her desk. These are eggs with the insides blown out and filled with confetti. Friends bop each other on the head with them during holidays and birthdays.

We took our *cascarones* to the cemetery, my first visit there. Miss D said she wanted to be buried under a mesquite tree, tough symbol of South Texas, and there she was. We cracked our *cascarones* on her tombstone, convinced she would have enjoyed it. I'm sure she did.

This column is an *abrazo* (embrace) for all you teachers who may never know how far your influence reaches. I think of Miss D often, and remain grateful for her hard lessons on the stewardship of words.

Miss D, it's that time of year and I'm not in Texas yet. Consider your tombstone bopped with a *cascaron* from a former feature editor who still misses you. It's a love tap.

MAY 6, 2006

"I AM A JELLY DOUGHNUT"

I'm going to learn German, thanks to Nick, the Renaissance Man from California.

I've known Nick for years. He's a retired electrical engineer who speaks English and Russian fluently, remembers German well enough to read it, and is taking Spanish classes now.

A few weeks ago, I wrote in an e-mail that I want to learn German as soon as I move someplace where it is taught. A week later, I got a package from Nick containing a set of CDs of advanced German instruction.

I had a good laugh, figuring he had used them for himself, then sent them as a gag to me, who learned all her German from *The Great Escape*—"jawohl, herr Oberst"—and words in history texts.

Boy howdy, was I wrong. This week, two more packages arrived. One is a monster German-English dictionary, and the other a course in basic German, along the lines of "Ist das ein Chevrolet?" "Ja, ist ein Chevrolet," repeated over and over.

I like the way German sounds; I also like the way all nouns are capitalized. Nice to know there's a Country giving Nouns the Respect due to them.

Someone else's language can be tricky. After the Berlin Wall went up, President John Kennedy went to Berlin and proclaimed in German: "I am a jelly doughnut." ("Ich bin ein Berliner.") Urban legend has made that phrase a blunder, but it isn't. Native Berliners wouldn't have said it quite that way, but they understood him perfectly.

My first foray into someone else's language came when I was a kid, living in Japan. We all learned some Japanese, but my sole memory now is a song. I'll sing it, if anyone's interested.

Even back then, I could see foreign languages had possibilities. From somewhere—probably the Department of Defense—Dad acquired a set of pamphlets teaching basic phrases useful in wartime.

In no time at all, I taught myself to say, "Halt, or I'll shoot," and "Dig a latrine here," in several languages. This dialogue never proved useful around my sister, Karen, though.

I studied Latin for three years in high school. I can still sing "Twinkle, Twinkle, Little Star" in Latin (just ask), and remember one line of poetry from Vergil's *Aeneid*.

What I really learned in Latin was the form and structure of Indo-European languages. Those classes in my Texas high school are the most important I ever took, because I use that information every day of the world.

I took Spanish my senior year in high school. I did it because I wanted to know what the Hispanic kids were saying in the halls during class. Turned out, they were just saying what the rest of us were saying in English. Give me a dope slap.

Señor Donaho taught Spanish. He was a delicate man confined to a wheelchair, never in good health, but enthusiastic about his subject. He would say something to us in Spanish, then say, "Repiten, ustedes." He had a dachshund named Señor Beethoven. ("Ist das ein Pooch?" "Ja, das ist ein Pooch.")

I studied Spanish in college, ending up with a minor. It's been years since I was moderately fluent, but I can still read Spanish. I have an abiding affection for Hispanics, particularly my grandchildren.

You never know when you'll need another language. For some weird reason, Americans seem to think that if they are in a foreign country, all they must do to be understood in English is to speak LOUD and slooow. (Dummkopf.)

Learn another language. Years ago in an airport, Jeremy came across a poor soul who was stalled at the metal detector. Jeremy was close enough to hear Portuguese, which he speaks. He leaped into a phone booth and came out, "Senhor Helpful American Portuguese Speaker."

The metal detector lady was trying to get the man to take off his belt and having little success. In Portuguese, Jeremy explained what she wanted, and the man quickly complied.

After he got through, he told my son, "I thought she wanted me to take off my pants."

Now I'm going to learn German. I don't plan to visit Germany anytime soon, but you never know. For old time's sake, I think I'll teach myself to say, "Dig a latrine here," and "Halt, or I'll shoot."

Especially that last one. They're our friends now, but I like to keep my options open.

MAY 11, 2006

AN EDUCATION OR A DEGREE?

I turned 59 on May 7, which means I have officially received "I don't care" status.

This means I'm old enough now to say exactly what I'm thinking, and sometimes it isn't pretty. Read at your own risk. If this column earns me irate rebuttals, refer to the above paragraph. Everything in it comes from personal experience and comments from educators.

I came across an article online last week titled, "More professors ban laptops in class." High time that happened. If there's a bigger time-waster among the immature in class these days, I'm not sure what it would be.

I love laptops. They have their place in the world, but they are not—repeat NOT—the friend of most students *in the classroom*, no matter what you may assume.

I taught history as an adjunct instructor at VCSU from 1997 to 1999, before all the classrooms were wired, and well before wireless made that wiring obsolete. In those unwired classrooms, students—the savvy ones—took notes by hand and actually made eye contact with me now and then. We exchanged opinions on the subject. I believe this is called the educational process.

I could see bad times ahead, though, particularly in the wired classrooms. Walking around the room, I noticed that quite a few students chose solitaire over Lewis and Clark.

You might argue that a business major doesn't need to know about Lewis and Clark. You'd be wrong. Part of the reason people used to go to school was to get an education, not just a degree.

A society's common knowledge tells a lot about that society. People who don't know their history, art, music, geography, literature, and culture are ignorant. They may emerge from college with a degree, but they're ignorant, just the same.

Stop Me If You've Read This One

My husband teaches at VCSU. He brings home stories of students devoting entire class periods to text messaging, playing games—poker is a huge offender on many campuses these days—and otherwise not attending to the matter at hand, which should be their education.

There are others who are even more blatant offenders. Not only are they in some parallel universe online, but they also have plugged wires into their ears so they can listen to music and tune their professor out entirely. Shame on them.

I know. You read this column to be entertained, and I like to oblige. I'm just deeply concerned that universities are cranking out illiterates.

The "Big" schools apparently are no better. I'm thinking of that huge scandal at Duke University involving the lacrosse team and the strippers. President Charles Kupchella at UND should be grateful his Fighting Sioux troubles are so small. (Don't even get me started on that logo business. Does it bother taxpayers that UND is spending time and money being so Jurassic? Change the name and move on. Grow up and live in the real world.)

What struck me about the Duke mess, proved bogus eventually, was the notorious e-mail one of the lacrosse players sent. It wasn't even what he said, even though it was scurrilous and vastly inappropriate. What caught my eye was his abysmal grammar and diction. And *Duke* let that clown enroll? He can't even compose a coherent sentence. I have to wonder who wrote his papers and took his tests for him.

Obviously, some students at top-tier universities are poorly educated, too. Universities take them, though, because many are athletes. (Really don't get me started on athletic scholarships to the ACT-score deficient.)

What's happened to education? Some kids still get it, thank goodness. I remember one at VCSU. His name was Jeremy Johnson (an excellent athlete, by the way), and he was in my Modern Europe class.

Jeremy, a history education major, was headed for student teaching the following semester. Right before class started one day, he asked me, "When you stand up there, do you ever feel as though you know enough?"

I remember my response. "Jeremy, I never feel as though I know enough. You just won the prize. You're educated."

Education is the humbling realization that you'll never know enough, no matter how many books you read, notes you take, or papers you write. And knowing that, you keep studying and learning. Jeremy understood.

I would pity undernourished students who text-message their way to a degree, except it would be pointless. They're too ignorant to know how ignorant they are.

SEPTEMBER 28, 2006

"ENOUGH!" SHE EXCLAIMED.

O h, goody! It's nearly October 1!
No, that's not some special holiday on Planet Grammaria requiring exclamation points. It's the end of my fiscal year for exclamation points!!

I was raised in a family where the US government paid my dad's salary. I worked for a few years in the National Park Service, another government entity. My modest government background taught me that if you don't use up allocated funding during the year, it will be slashed from next year's budget.

It's the same with grammar. I never use all my exclamation points in the fiscal grammar year. If my verbs or the occasional adjective aren't exciting enough, an exclamation point will only inject false enthusiasm, the kind cheerleaders exude when the score is 78-0 and fans are sidling toward the exits, making no eye contact.

As October 1 approaches, I find myself in the ticklish position of being forced to use up those pesky points. I don't want them to disappear entirely from my writing budget, so I must find a home for them here and there before that deadline!

I don't like them. Maybe they're not part of my Scots DNA. People with an ancestral memory of damp, bog, chapped knees, and haggis (horrors!) probably aren't inclined to look kindly upon perky punctuation. More for us the sledgehammer of a semicolon.

Ah, the semicolon. People who use the semicolon are few. Those of us who do use it correctly are of above average intelligence. That's the way it is. Sorry!

I admit I did use more exclamation points when I was a teenager. I think I even drew big, fat circles to dot the *i*'s. I blame that on teenage angst that requires us to "find ourselves." I quickly found it looked stupid and quit.

I was nurtured in high school by Jean Dugat, my first and only journalism instructor. Miss D believed in the verb's ability to liven any paragraph. She looked with no favor on the word *very*, either. To this day, I weigh the use of that word with more deliberation than most world leaders devote to world peace. Want a *very*? I have plenty.

The right word matters. Every year around February 24, Miss D would put Lieutenant Colonel William Travis's last message from the Alamo on her bulletin board. We expected it; this was Texas, for crying out loud.

I think now there was more to it than just a patriotic message. As I reread Travis's last letter, I am impressed—maybe humbled—by his clear use of language. Was Miss D trying to teach us something?

Here's the text. Travis was fond of the dash, but that's okay. He knew he was going to die. Maybe he was using up his fiscal year of dashes.

To the People of the world & all Americans in the world –

Fellow citizens & compatriots—I am besieged by a thousand or more of the Mexicans under Santa Anna—I have sustained a continual Bombardment & cannonade for 24 hours & have not lost a man— The enemy has demanded a surrender at discretion, otherwise, the garrison are to be put to the sword, if the fort is taken—I have answered the demand with a cannon shot, & our flag still waves proudly from the walls—I shall never surrender or retreat.

Then, I call on you in the name of Liberty, of patriotism & everything dear to the American character, to come to our aid, with all dispatch—The enemy is receiving reinforcements daily & will no doubt increase to three or four thousand in four or five days.

If this call is neglected, I am determined to sustain myself as long as possible & die like a soldier who never forgets what is due to his own honor & that of his country—Victory or death.

William Barret Travis, Lt. Col. Comdt

Wow. What a cool customer Travis was. Everything is about to go to pieces and there is not an exclamation point in sight.

Now and then, though, only an exclamation point will do. Consider General Anthony McAuliffe's written response on December 21, 1944, when the German command demanded his surrender at Bastogne in the Battle of the Bulge: "Nuts!"

Perfect. Thank goodness McAuliffe hadn't run out of exclamation points. That's why I hoard them. No telling when you might need one. Just one.

DECEMBER 14, 2006

MARCUS LOVES SPENDUSA

I'm a sucker for Roman history. One fascinating thing about Pompeii is the graffiti found on the city walls while the Roman resort was being excavated from the lava flow of Mount Vesuvius. It tells us much about everyday life, and even more about human nature.

Here are some favorites—found on walls and gates, and outside bars and cafes—translated from Latin:

"Marcus loves Spendusa."

"The finance officer of the emperor Nero says this food is poison."

"Celadus the Thracian gladiator is the delight of all the girls."

"On April 20, I gave a cloak to be washed. On May 7, a headband. On May 8, two tunics."

"Cruel Lalagus, why do you not love me?"

"If anyone does not believe in Venus, they should gaze at my girlfriend."

"Samius to Cornelius: go hang yourself!"

"O walls, you have held up so much tedious graffiti that I am amazed that you have not already collapsed in ruin."

I have my own graffiti board. It's my writing board, a metal stand by my computer. I've had it about 20 years, and I've taped some pithy statements on it that caught my eye. Someday I'll will this to the kid in the family who writes the most. The board is useful, tells a lot about me, and about what I was thinking at certain times.

Here's a poem by Steve Cornett, which I taped to the board when my kids were teenagers:

If children moved away at twelve,
We'd wring our hands and grieve;
Thus God provided teen-age years
To make us glad they leave.

This yellowed newspaper item probably went on the board before 1990, because of the reference to West Germany.

(Headline) "*Relocating? Chad is bad.*

The world's worst place to live is Chad, followed by Afghanistan, Burkina Faso and Ethiopia, says International Living magazine, sort of a place-rated almanac of countries.

The best places, the magazine found, are the United States, Canada, West Germany and Australia."

Don't know where this one came from, but it's certainly a philosophy I live by: "*Don't put off 'til tomorrow what you can do today. That way, if you liked it, you can do it again tomorrow.*"

Here's a personal favorite by historians Will and Ariel Durant, written in a forward to one of their books: *All in all, in life and in history, we have found so many good men and women that we have quite lost faith in the wickedness of mankind.*

Here's a quote from Ray Bradbury, and it's one all writers should memorize: *I held the bird in my hands, one hand cupped over the other. I could not feel the weight of the bird, and would not have known it was there or even alive except I could feel its heart beating. So it is with a good story or poem. You should feel the heartbeat, without feeling the weight of what you are reading.*

I came across this one when we lived in Louisiana. Life was bad, and I was desperate to be elsewhere:

Big Horn Mountain Retreat. A unique 75-acre tract nestled against the Wyoming State Elk Refuge, this property is bordered on its other three sides by two large ranches in strong hands. Perfectly sited and beautifully landscaped 10-year-old log home provides a comfortable, year-round or summer retreat. The ranch overlooks rolling hay meadows and beautiful, spring-fed draws of aspen, with bold red cliffs which reflect the sunlight. This is a rare opportunity to buy into one of Wyoming's most beautiful and closely held mountain valleys.

I can't tell you how many times that little scrap on my writing board has sustained me through tough times.

There's this truism, from Ellis Peter's novel, *One Corpse Too Many*. Father Cadfael, a 12th-century monk, is speaking to Shrewsbury's undersheriff, Hugh Beringar:

You did the work that fell to you, and did it well. God disposes all. From the highest to the lowest extreme of a man's scope, wherever justice and retribution can reach him, so can grace.

I'll conclude with this paragraph from the Orlando *Sentinel*, which has amused me through the years (we already know I am too easily amused):

What do you know about Holland? British wit Alan Coren wrote: "Apart from cheese and tulips, the main product of the country is advocaat, a drink made from lawyers."

And Marcus still loves Spendusa.

FEBRUARY 8, 2007

JOURNALISM IN A FREE SOCIETY

Pay close attention. I do not like Nazis. I don't like anything about them. Never have. Never will.

Here's what I am passionate about: Freedom of the press.

Here's something that worries me: People who only want news they like in their newspaper. As a point of fact, Adolf Hitler, Benito Mussolini, Josef Stalin, and Idi Amin insisted their newspapers print only news they liked.

Several weeks ago, the *Times-Record* received an e-mail from John Bowles, who said he would be in town with his "entourage." He offered to provide an interview, because he's running for president.

I told our publisher I'd be interested in interviewing him. It's news, after all. Journalists have a duty to keep people informed of the good, the bad, the ugly, and he was coming to town.

This semester, I'm teaching Communications 344 at Valley City State University. It's a course in reporting and feature writing. When I heard the Nazis were coming, I contacted VCSU's academic vice president and told him I wanted to invite Bowles to my class, so my students could interview him, too.

We weren't able to have Bowles on campus for one reason only: Bowles refuses to go anywhere without his "security force," and the goons couldn't be included in the invitation to my class.

I interviewed Bowles elsewhere. I was polite. He was polite. I knew Bowles would say stuff that showed how pathetic and purposeless his warped point of view is.

Bowles did exactly that. I reported his actual words on the Holocaust, and his "solution" to what he terms the "African-American problem," confident that readers would understand unbiased reporting in a free society. In retrospect, that may have been my mistake.

If it's any comfort to all of you who are fuming, it made my skin crawl to sit in the same room with those smug, evil men. I wanted to go home and take a shower when they finished.

My own dislike wouldn't have excused me from interviewing them, even though I object to everything they stand for. Journalists can't choose to just interview people they admire.

My job was to report, in an unbiased way, what Bowles said. This is called journalism. It's practiced all over the world, but only in free societies where citizens may think and form their own opinions.

There is one question I wish I had asked Bowles; it's one all readers in Valley City may wish to consider. I'm still kicking myself that I did not ask it, even though I am not so stupid as to think he would have given me a truthful answer.

It's this: Bowles and his two security guards came to North Dakota specifically to visit Valley City and Fargo. Why just here?

Are there people around here who subscribe to the views of the American Nazi Party? Is that why he was here? Does he have enough supporters in this area that he felt Valley City was fertile ground for more recruits? I'm embarrassed I didn't pick up on that, because that worries me even more than people who think newspapers shouldn't print stuff they disagree with. Why were they here?

It's your right to protest anything you read in the paper, but by no means does that article mean the *Times-Record* was "endorsing" Bowles. I was reporting the news. Nothing more.

I had an experience once with knee-jerk reactions when I lived in Louisiana. It was in a Sunday school class, of all places. I was teaching the class and trying to explain some Old Testament unpleasantness by comparing it to something Union General Ulysses Grant did once.

What I said wasn't complimentary of Grant, but I forgot my audience—Southerners apparently still smarting from losing the Civil War more than 130 years ago. Some didn't hear one word beyond "Grant." All my reasonable explanation would have been like a whisper on the wind. One of the class members objected, and that was the last time I taught Sunday school in Louisiana.

This is not an apology for writing that article. It's an explanation of why I did it. If journalists are not allowed to report the news, then you might as well kiss democracy good-bye, because we'll wake up to the kind of police state Bowles wants to see in our communities.

FEBRUARY 22, 2007

ALL MY YOUNG AND RESTLESS CHILDREN

I've discovered the cure for the common winter. I was eating breakfast Saturday, and reading *The Forum*, depressed at yet another day of negative weather numbers even lower than I can count, and asking myself why I live here.

On the back page of the weekly TV supplement, I came across this sentence:

"Everyone was devastated when Dixie died after being poisoned by the Satin Slayer."

Wide awake, I read some more. "Natalie told Luke that Faith has been binging and purging." Then: "Mimi lied to Roman that she found the bones Bonnie had stolen."

I was in heaven. Where has this been all my life? I laughed and kept reading. "Frank threw Alan in jail after Cassie got him to admit he tried to have Jonathan killed, but Tammy died instead."

Well, I feel bad for Tammy, but jeez louise, what *is* this?

Welcome to the weekly digest of the soap operas. If there's a more hilarious page in the newspaper, I can't imagine what it is. I mean, the funnies don't exactly amuse anymore. Dr. Rex Morgan's amazingly young and nubile wife is battling meth dealers, and Mary Worth is worried about facial hair and low estrogen. Not fun.

That back page is worth the whole paper. I've been smiling all day through sub-zero temperatures, hands so rough and cracked I could probably sand furniture with them, and my Camry making more clicks and chortles than a whole pod of whales.

Thank you, *All My Children*, *Young and the Restless*, and *Days of Our Lives*. I've never watched soap operas and don't intend to start, but I'm curious: How do the actors manage to deliver such fraught lines—Tammy's dead, Willow's hunting for Claire, Gasparro lied about finding a tumor—with straight faces? That's some acting.

The names are cool, too, not ordinary names like Phil, or Ed, or Janet. These amazing (and probably beautiful) people have names like Willow, Belle, Starr, Cole, Skye, and Rex. Carla's pretty dull, isn't it? I think I'll call myself Cerise Latour.

These are tough women. In the summary of "The Young and the Restless," Sheila got Maggie to let her out of a makeshift cell, then: "Sheila knocked Maggie out, and later knocked Paul out when he returned." If that's not enough, Sheila shot Maggie in the stomach, too. I feel I've accomplished a lot if I get my panty hose on straight for church, but this Sheila's going around kicking serious butt. Oh no. "Someone posing as Carmen is terrorizing Dru." Should I worry?

I don't know what these people do for a living, but they have time to get in trouble. Maybe it's carpentry; someone had to build that makeshift cell. "General Hospital" probably has something to do with medicine. One can hope, anyway, especially some guy named Alcazar (maybe he was conceived in that palace in Spain), who "had a seizure after he told Skye the briefcase in the vault is set to explode, but lost consciousness before revealing the code needed to prevent the explosion."

I'm not making this up. As a well-seasoned, published novelist, I'm in awe of writers who can cram such event into one five-day period. They must be a jolly bunch; how can they not laugh at all this earnest nonsense?

My life is so dull. I get up too early, go to work too early, work too hard, rush home and fix dinner, then usually work at night, too. No one wants to know the days of my life. The only young and the restless I've known were my kids when they were cooped up indoors during Wyoming winters. Silly goose, I know I have only one life to live. I'm living it as a nearsighted, fluffy woman with thinning hair, a stammer, and flat feet. But hey, it's a cool enough life.

I can make it through winter now. All I have to do is read that back page of the Forum's TV section. Here's this one: "Emily was disgusted with herself after she slept with a strange man, Steve."

Shame on you, Emily. If the other summaries are any indication, Steve is probably your a) half-brother raised in the Amazon by Yanomami Indians b) landlord wearing Groucho glasses and fake nose c) Aussie window washer whose sister Sheila is going to knock you out.

Emily, maybe some guy named Dung Heap or Strip Badley will come along and let you out of that makeshift cell.

APRIL 5, 2007

EASTER EGGS: A CONFESSION

News flash: A satellite has pinpointed seven spots on Mars that scientists think are caves. The scientists are full of theories about the Martian caves. Important stuff.

Here's what intrigues me: The scientists named those caves after loved ones—Dena, Chloe, Wendy, Annie, Abbey, Nikki, and Jeanne.

It's nice to know that in the rarefied scientific world, people still name places for their sweeties. Of course, Chloe could be a basset hound.

Naming things for others isn't new. Think of Meriwether Lewis, who named the Marias River after his cousin, Maria Wood. Too bad the map is mostly full now.

Here's what I do: I name characters in my novels after loved ones, friends, or people to whom I owe money. (I'm joking. I've never named a character Wells or Fargo.)

One novel, *Miss Billings Treads the Boards*, I named after Billings, Montana, a city I like, partly because I have Trask relatives in and around there. That novel is also peopled with Broussards, Sheffields, and Graysons: friends in Louisiana, where I was living when I wrote that book. (Don't writers have fun?)

I also use characteristics. All writers do; we work with what we know. *Marian's Christmas Wish*, which I wrote in 1989, is about a whole family of interesting children. There is Marian, of course, and her sister, Ariadne. Their older brother, Percy, is a diplomat, at work in Belgium with the British delegation on the Treaty of Ghent, which ended the War of 1812. There is Alistair, the rascal of a younger brother sent home from Oxford to "rusticate." (Uh oh. Expelled.)

The Wynswiches are my real children, but with different names. Percy is the practical older brother—Jeremy—and Alistair, the fun-loving rascal, is Sam. Marian and Ariadne are a combination of my three daughters as they were 18 years ago: mature one moment, children the next.

In the novel, Percy comes home at Christmas, just before the treaty is actually signed, but after his role in it is done. He brings with him a fellow diplomat, Sir William Clinghorn, who had heard Percy talk about his lovely sister, Ariadne, and who is interested in marrying her.

Sir William is older, fat, and stupid, but he is wealthy. Such an arranged marriage—common then—would revive the Wynswich family's fortune, sadly depleted by their now-dead spendthrift father. Ariadne is in love with someone else, though, and the plot revolves from there.

Here is my other side: Sir William has the quirks and irritating habits of my boss then, a man for whom I had little admiration and no respect. I cordially despised him.

I needed my job; it paid well and I couldn't afford to quit. But I could put that toxic boss into *Marian's Christmas Wish* as Sir William, who becomes a laughingstock by the time the novel ends.

That's what I did. Few knew, and I never mentioned a word of this to my boss, because—refer to the previous paragraph.

I didn't know it at the time, but these little private "jokes" hidden in books, software, and paintings are called "Easter eggs." More writers do this than you can imagine. It is way of thanking and honoring people we love, or making fun of those we dislike. I've done this in nearly every book I have written.

I study people; all novelists do. We can't help ourselves. You'll never know what I'm thinking, and I'm fine with that. If one of your quirks, bad habits, or endearing qualities shows up in a novel, or I use your name somewhere, so it goes.

Don't try to outguess me. Some villains (I don't use many) are just villains because the story needs a villain. Others are people I really don't like.

Studying people is an art form. Some readers have told me they like my ordinary characters in fiction who, when hit with a painful load, learn how to square their shoulders and bear up as best they can. I know courageous people who do precisely that. I hope you know who you are.

Of the buffoons and silly ladies in my novels, you won't know, because people seldom see themselves as others see them. That's the writer's gift and burden. Almost without realizing it, I think: How can I use this person? And I do. Happy Easter egg.

APRIL 26, 2007

E. P., WRITE HOME

"Your call is important to us." The only thing sillier than that sentence is "One size fits all."

I was trying to call someone here in town who runs a major business, to make an appointment for an interview. I had an e-mail, but it bounced back. When I called the business, the menu choice got me nowhere except back where I started. I tried it several times, operating on the idiot principle that if I tried the same thing enough times, something might change. Silly wabbit.

Between my admiration for a company that makes communication impossible—so therefore must get a lot done between 8:00 a.m. and 5:00 p.m.—and my frustration at being completely stymied, I knew I'd be writing a column about this.

Remember the not-so-distant past when the answering machine was the new kid on the block? Remember how irritating it was to get the answering machine instead of the person you wanted to talk to?

Fast forward to 2007. Now I get frustrated when I don't get an answering machine. When the phone just rings and rings, I think, "Why don't these doofuses have an answering machine?"

Even worse, sometimes I actually get a human, when all I wanted to do was leave a message. How awkward is that, having to talk to someone?

Dances with Wolves was a dumb movie, but it had one of my favorite scenes of all times in it. Remember that sequence when John Dunbar is heading West with a load of supplies, and he and his driver come across the skeleton pincushioned full of arrows?

The driver looks at the skeleton and announces, "Someone back East is probably wondering, 'Why don't he write?'"

I figure lots of people have written lots of letters never received. It's a fiction writer's handy plot device. Shakespeare used it to good effect in

Romeo and Juliet. I used it once in a short story, and it worked well, too.

A few years ago when I did that big Fort Buford research project for the State Historical Society, I came across an interesting letter, dated November 26, 1878, from the post surgeon, P. H. Harvey, to the post adjutant.

Harvey wrote he and the other post surgeon had ridden out to look at the skeletal remains of a man found by two soldiers who had been hunting. "Nothing remained but the bony skeleton and several articles of clothing, very much decayed and fallen into pieces," Harvey wrote.

He said there was a knife handle with the initials, E. P., near the body. When Harvey put the "bones of the head" together, it became obvious that cause of death was from a gunshot wound to the forehead.

From the direction the skeleton's rifle and pistol were both pointing, Harvey surmised the death was either a suicide or an accident and not a murder, particularly since money was found beneath the skeleton, about where a back pocket would be located.

The man was dressed in military clothing. Harvey collected affidavits from the two sergeants who had found the body, and with his own letter, made copies and forwarded them to other army garrisons in the vicinity. According to the return endorsements, no one claimed him.

I've thought about that man a time or two, since then. In one of my short stories in "Here's to the Ladies: Stories of the Frontier Army," one character comments to another something like, "With a good horse, a rifle, and a new name, anyone can make a fresh start in the West." It happened often enough.

I've wondered if someone back East missed that man. There are so many threads that just never get tied up in this life. It frustrates me occasionally that my publisher always wants a happy ending, but I suppose that's the way we like things: all tidy and understandable.

Real life isn't so convenient. I'm certain Captain Harvey had the bones boxed and interred in the cemetery at Fort Buford. Several of the grave markers have "Unknown" written on them, so "Bones" obviously wasn't the only guy without a name.

When Fort Buford closed, most of the military remains were relocated to Custer Battlefield National Cemetery in Montana. I guess you can be unknown just about anywhere.

I still think about him, wondering if some mother, sister, or wife went to her own grave, worrying still, wishing she knew.

Write to someone tonight, OK? Or leave a message.

MAY 10, 2007

NO PENCILS, BOOKS OR DIRTY LOOKS

The combination of spring and school does something to students. Late-night skivvy-dipping in Concordia College's pond after graduation comes to mind. What amused me—and doubtless, others—was when the grads scattered as cops arrived, leaving behind wallets and other forms of ID.

Here's my question: Should students too dumb to grab their IDs have been awarded diplomas? I say, retain them for another semester so they can take a 300-level course in Horse Sense.

School antics. My sister, Karen, remembered one from her sophomore year at Cody High School in Cody, Wyoming.

During Christmas break in 1960, several enterprising guys managed to swipe all the books from lockers, classrooms, and the school library and hide them in the old building's attic.

The culprits were eventually uncovered and the books restored. I don't know what the punishment was, but hopefully, it didn't go beyond 30 lashes and weevily bread for a semester. Stealing (read, relocating) books is a stroke of comic genius. I mean, who does that?

Like students everywhere, students at Brigham Young University, my alma mater, have a fine sense of the ridiculous. In front of the science building is a statue of Karl Maeser, German-born educator and president of Brigham Young Academy from 1876 to 1892.

There he stands, a dignified sight in his frock coat, a book in his right hand, and his left hand behind his back.

One morning as I hurried to class, I glanced up as I passed Brother Maeser and noticed he was clutching nylons in that left hand. Karl, say it isn't so! On winter mornings, he sometimes held a snowball.

I realize that's pretty tame, but we Mormons don't generally go underwear-dipping in college ponds. It's not recommended anywhere in BYU's famously strict dress code.

There's a pond in front of BYU's Smoot Building, presided over by a statue of Brigham Young himself. Invariably, toward the end of spring semester, someone used to dump detergent in Brother Brigham's pond.

I can't speak for the old gentleman himself, but I never thought he would have been unduly upset with all the bubbles. He understood youth. One of his memorable statements was: "Any man over 21 and unmarried is a menace to society."

My favorite school pranks are in a delightful book, *The Lawrenceville Stories*, by Owen Johnson, himself a graduate of that prestigious New Jersey prep school. Written around 1910, but telling of an earlier era, the stories describe the hijinks of the Tennessee Shad, Doc MacNooder, the Walladoo Bird, the Varmint, Lovely Mead, and the Prodigious Hickey.

I always think of Hickey as finals approach at colleges and high schools.

The lively, lark-minded William Hicks had run his professors ragged for years. Finally, after the dismantling and reassembling of a professor's bed on the baseball diamond, it was too much. As usual, there was no way to connect Hickey to the evil deed, but Hickey it was.

Fed up, the Doctor summoned Hickey to his office.

"Well, Hicks, we're going to let you go."

"Beg your pardon, sir," said Hickey, *smiling frankly back, "you said . . ."*

"We're going to let you take a vacation."

"Me?"

"You."

Hickey stood a long moment, open-mouthed, staring. *"Do you mean to say . . . that I am expelled?"*

"Not expelled, said the Doctor suavely. *"We don't like that word; we're going to let you go, that's all."*

"For what reason?" said Hickey defiantly.

"For no reason at all," answered the Doctor. *"There is no reason, there can be no reason, Hicks. We're just naturally going to make up our minds to part with you."*

The Doctor cataloged a list of complaints and concluded with this delightful passage: *"We have, we fear, been forgetting the main object of our life here—to study a little."*

But he reassured Hickey: *"We're parting with you, Hicks, because we feel we no longer have anything to teach you."*

The Doctor is regretful, but firm, as he orders Hickey to leave on the evening train because, *"We have lost a great deal of sleep lately."*

It's spring. Raise a cheer to carefree youth, sleepless as they cram for finals. Just don't leave your ID behind as you celebrate, eh?

JULY 3, 2007

I HEREBY DECLARE

Before David and Olga Silverman left town for greener pastures in Missouri, they held a yard sale. I'm no yard sale person, but we happened to be at their house. I bought a real gem: A book titled *Pass the US Citizenship Exam*. Olga is a native of Latvia, and she was studying for US citizenship.

This is a great little book, with its concise explanations of American history and government. Also included in what I purchased for a dollar was *Learn about the United States: Quick Civics Lessons*. Published by the US Citizenship and Immigration Services, it contains 96 questions and brief answers. As I looked through both booklets, I started wondering how many people who were born here could answer these questions.

I knew I had better be able to answer them, or else my old department chair from the University of Louisiana—Monroe would probably show up on my doorstep and whip my master's degree in American history out of my sweaty palms.

I wasn't too worried. I'm the geek who stays awake on long, solo car trips by giving a lecture to imaginary students—maybe they're lurking in the back seat—on Grant's Vicksburg campaign of 1863. I usually begin from the point where he and his Yankee army crossed the Mississippi River from the Louisiana side between Grand Gulf and Bruinsburg, marched east to Jackson, Mississippi, then fought a series of battles going west to Vicksburg, followed by a six-week siege. Great stuff; I give a good car lecture. You're welcome to ride along and take notes. Yeah, it's dumb, but this keeps me awake while I drive, since I'm lecturing and not listening. What about it? Can you pass the test for US citizenship? Here are some random questions that might be asked during the citizenship interview:

- What are the colors of our flag?

- What do the stars on the flag represent?
- What country did we fight during the Revolutionary War?
- Who elects the president of the United States?
- Who becomes president if both the President and the Vice President die?
- What is the Constitution?
- How many amendments are there to the Constitution?
- What are the three branches of our government?
- Describe each branch.
- What makes up Congress?
- Name two senators from your state.
- How many voting members are in the House of Representatives?
- What are the duties of the Supreme Court?
- What is the Bill of Rights?
- Who is Chief Justice of the Supreme Court?
- Name the 13 original states.
- Who said, "Give me liberty or give me death"?
- Name three major countries that were our enemies in World War II.
- Who was the main writer of the Declaration of Independence?
- What did the Emancipation Proclamation do?
- What kind of government does the United States have?

And so it goes, on through a list of basic, common knowledge kind of questions. It's just bare bones stuff everyone should know, in order to function as a US citizen. After the test, there are questions about yourself, your family, your employment, how you feel about things, and why you want to become a US citizen anyway. You'll have to certify to your moral character.

If everything is in order, you'll stand up, raise your hand, and take this Oath of Allegiance, a privilege if ever there was one:

I hereby declare, on oath, that I absolutely and entirely renounce and abjure all allegiance and fidelity to any foreign price, potentate, state or sovereignty, of whom or which I have heretofore been a subject or citizen; that I will support and defend the Constitution and laws of the United States when required by law; that I will bear true faith and allegiance to the same; that I will bear arms on behalf of the United States when required by law; that I will perform noncombatant service in the Armed Forces of the United States when required by law; that I will perform work of national importance under civilian direction when required by law; and that I take this obligation freely, without any mental reservation or purpose of evasion, so help me God.

Happy Fourth of July. (Incidentally, Vicksburg surrendered to Grant on July 4. Ouch.)

AUGUST 7, 2007
PINK BIKINIS AND BAROMETERS

All right, everybody, listen up: Where were you on the night of August 1? I don't want to get all surly around the mouth, but something in our neighborhood was rustled during the wee hours, and we'd like to solve the crime.

Some miscreant in town is running around with a lady's sequined pink bikini, extra large, that doesn't belong to her or him. Said garment was swiped or otherwise pilfered from the clothesline in Jerry and BJ Edwardson's front yard on Fourth Street Southwest.

You drive-by types have probably noticed BJ's clothesline. For the last five years or so, she celebrates the seasons by hanging appropriate clothing. (The idea came from her sister, Nancy, in Oregon.) Last spring, when the weather seemed to change every fifteen minutes, she had a fur coat on the line for the snowy days, then draped a raincoat over the fur coat when the snow turned liquid. Hunting season gets it due, as well, with camouflage and orange. The only season I haven't seen observed on BJ's line is construction season. Maybe she'll hang some orange and white cones next spring.

The bikini is gone. BJ wants the bikini back on the line, no questions asked. Just hang it quietly on the line again, and no one will get hurt.

Ah, the creative spirit. Here's one of my favorite examples, courtesy of Alexander Calandra, PhD, Washington University in St. Louis, Missouri. Calandra was a distinguished professor, an expert in the field of science education. He died March 8, 2006, at the age of 95. In spite of his numerous scientific and academic achievements, he is probably best remembered for his essay "The Barometer Story."

Calandra was called upon by a frustrated colleague to arbitrate an exam question. The teacher was about to give his student a zero for failure to properly determine the height of a building using a barometer.

Calandra's words: "The student's answer was, 'Take the barometer to the top of the building, attach a long rope to it, lower the barometer to the street, then bring it up, measuring the length of the rope.'"

Calandra pointed out to the instructor that the student "had a strong case for full credit, since he had answered the question completely and correctly." Calandra also knew that if the student received full credit, it would result in a high grade in a physics course, even though the answer indicated no knowledge of physics.

Calandra asked the student to provide another answer that exhibited some knowledge of physics. The student agreed, sitting in thought for five minutes. When Calandra chided him for wasting everyone's time, the student assured him there were many ways to solve the problem; he was just trying to choose the best one.

In the minute remaining, the student wrote: "Take the barometer to the top of the building and lean over the edge of the roof. Drop the barometer, timing its fall with a stopwatch. Using the formula, sx1/2 AT squared, calculate the height of the building."

After this answer, the instructor gave up and allowed full credit. Calandra was intrigued, and followed the student from the classroom, asking if he knew of other ways to determine the height of the building using a barometer. The student had many ways: "Take the barometer out on a sunny day and measure the height of the barometer, the length of its shadow, and the length of the shadow of the building, and by the use of simple proportion, determine the height of the building."

More answers poured out. A person could climb the stairs and mark off the length of the barometer on the wall, which would give the height of the building in barometer units. A more sophisticated method involved a pendulum.

Here's my favorite. Take the barometer to the building's superintendent and say, "Dear Mr. Superintendent, here I have a fine barometer. If you will tell me the height of the building, I will give you this barometer."

Calandra then asked the student if he actually knew the "approved" answer to the problem. The student assured him he did, but he was tired of instructors trying to teach him how to think, as though there was only one solution to a problem.

BJ, I don't know if you'll get back that pink bikini. Perhaps the thief has something creative in mind. Should we be keeping an eye on the fig-leafed statues in Vangstad Auditorium?

OCTOBER 23, 2007

THE LOVE DOCTOR IS IN

Years ago, I received my first Golden Spur Award from Western Writers of America for a short story. (I have two of those suckers. All I need is a horse.) At an awards luncheon for finalists, I sat across from novelist Frank Roderus, who used to write for Doubleday. I was starting out in the writing biz, and he told me this: "Carla, some day you'll hate your editor."

"Oh, no, not *moi*," I assured him, all dewy-eyed and idealistic. Well darned if Frank wasn't right. I really should tell him that yes, indeedy, I hate my editor. Actually, I've hated several of them.

Perhaps that's too strong a word. Loathe? Despise? Would not pick her up if she were wandering in a bad neighborhood? Would send her out minus her burka and wearing lipstick in a country full of Taliban fans? All the above. Die, editor, die.

Welcome to the wonderful world of fiction. I wish I had a quarter for every time someone has told me, "I want to write a novel." No, you don't. It's hard work and when you're done, you have to turn the project over to the "expert," your editor. Granted, editors occasionally offer useful advice on how to make something better, and I've been glad for that advice. My problem lately is book titles.

I write for Harlequin now. Before you roll your eyes and snicker, I'll tell you what I tell others: "If it's so easy, you do it." Besides, they pay well enough and are distributed everywhere.

Last fall, I wrote the first installment of a series about the British Channel Fleet during the bad old days of the Napoleonic War. The hero was a frigate captain named Oliver Worthy. I called the novel *Worthy*, because of his name, and also because the heroine—a charming creature readers will love—had some gnawing doubts about her own worthiness for his affections.

My editor didn't like the title, because it wasn't romance-y enough. I can live with that, except that she didn't have any better ideas. We hashed around a few titles, and ended up with the tepid title, *Marrying the Captain*. I quickly wrote book two of the series, which is about a surgeon in the Royal Navy and the sister of the love interest in *Marrying the Captain*. Since it has a medical setting, and this sister has a few issues, too, I called it *Do No Harm*, which seemed perfect for the medical/nautical theme.

No dice. This second book is due to come out in June 2009, and Harlequin must, MUST have a title now. When we decided on *Marrying the Captain*, months ago, my editor said that logically, we should call the next one *Marrying the Surgeon*. That percolated through her brain for six months, and now it won't do, because it sounds "too modern"—never mind that navy surgeons go back at least to the 17th century. Sigh.

"How about *Marrying the Royal Surgeon*?" she asked me today. "No," I e-mailed her. "We could say Royal Navy Surgeon and that would be correct." "Can't do," she e-mailed back. "It's too long."

I resisted the urge to write, "How about *No Drums, No Trumpets*, because it doesn't have any drums or trumpets?" It's an old writer's joke, but I didn't e-mail that, because I am basically kind, and I want to keep writing books. Besides, she might have thought I was being nasty, which I was.

Anyway, there I was, frustrated and hating my editor. My daughter Liz called and I told her this whole story. We laughed a lot, because we came up with some great titles that a newspaper in North Dakota won't print. We said good-bye and hung up.

Liz called me back with the perfect title. I should put her on the payroll. "Mom, call it *The Love Doctor Is In*," she said. We laughed some more. I still hate my editor, but I have a column now, so it wasn't all bad.

I don't know what the title will be, and I'm writing book three, which involves a Royal Marine this time. I think I'll call it *Gomer Pyle: Royal Marine*, and let it go at that, because they won't like whatever I title it. Nah, you don't want to write a novel. Editors are the spawn of Satan.

HISTORY AND TRADITION

DECEMBER 30, 2004

THE LITTLE TOWN THAT COULD

The can-do spirit is alive and well in America. I'm thinking of the $4,000 that students at Agassiz Middle School in Fargo raised in a "coin war" to send to a school in Florida devastated by hurricanes Charley, Frances, Ivan, and Jeanne (pick one or all four). I'm also thinking of the lady in Minot who is making 29 fleece blankets for the soldiers in her son's unit in Iraq. Or the thousands of cookies a Minot sorority is making for sailors on the USS *Mobile Bay*. Or Operation Iraqi Backpack right here.

I'm thinking of Linda Gross of Encino, California, who, with four families, was vacationing in Phuket, Thailand, when the tsunami slammed ashore this week. Instead of bolting for the airport—tourists have the luxury of doing that—these American families bought food, water, and clothing, got in a van, and headed for harder hit areas around their untouched hotel. They've done that several times now, except for one of their number—a doctor—who just walked into the nearest hospital and started working.

When the CNN interviewer asked Linda Gross when they were planning to leave, she said that the families have decided to stay past their departure date and keep working. Said Gross, "It's a teaching moment for our children. We were so blessed. We have to help others who need us."

We have to help others who need us.

On December 17, 1941, townsfolk in North Platte, Nebraska, gathered at the Union Pacific Depot. It was only ten days after Pearl Harbor, and nine days after the declaration of war. Someone in town had heard a rumor that Company D of their local National Guard unit, which had been training in Arkansas, was heading their way. They brought presents and other goodies to give their boys who were traveling west on one of the first of many troop trains, bound for war. Moms and dads planned to do some rapid visiting with their sons in the ten minutes the train would stop. Who knew when, or if, they would see them again?

Company D showed up on schedule, but it was a National Guard unit from Kansas, not Nebraska. After a moment of confusion and disappointment, someone in the hometown crowd yelled, "Let's give it to these boys!"

And they did. What was born that day was the North Platte Canteen, an amazing bit of love and sacrifice from one town in Nebraska, which took up the mission to mother a nation's sons and daughters headed for war. Before World War II ended in 1945, some six million armed forces personnel came to know and cherish the generosity of a town with nothing, really, to give to the war effort except its heart and soul.

On the day after that train mix-up, Rae Wilson wrote a letter to the local newspaper, urging the community to run a canteen and meet every troop train. Wilson wrote, "I say, get back of our sons and other mothers' sons 100 percent. Let's do something and do it in a hurry! We can help this way when we can't help any other way."

In a scant week, the town organized and opened its heart to soldiers, sailors, and Marines on Christmas Day, 1941. For the next 51 months, the canteen provided around-the-clock food, magazines, entertainment, and general good cheer. A typical day began at 5:00 a.m., with the arrival of the first train. At first, volunteers prepared food at a nearby hotel, and "platform girls" offered free food, cigarettes, candy, gum, and smiles right there, even in wintry Nebraska. They didn't stop until the last train had left. (During one amazing day at the height of the war, the canteen served 2,000 armed forces personnel on four trains within a half-hour period.)

William Jeffers, president of the Union Pacific Railroad, quickly dedicated the public dining room at the depot to the canteen. Its capacity of 600 people was generally large enough to comfortably serve the soldiers who detrained to stretch their legs, and discovered—to their delight—that they were in the capable hands of mothers, daughters, wives, and sisters with loved ones of their own fighting in Europe, North Africa, and the Pacific.

In a time of stringent rationing, and with America's heartland still struggling to emerge from the Great Depression, the amount of money and food raised for the canteen was nothing short of miraculous. Individuals, clubs, and area businesses provided money and sponsored fundraisers. By the time the war ended, over 300 organizations in 125 surrounding towns had made the North Platte canteen their personal project. The folks of North Platte could proudly declare that no state or federal funds ever came their way, unless you counted the five dollars that President Franklin D. Roosevelt sent, when he heard about the canteen.

What a menu. The daily fare—every bite free—included sandwiches, fried chicken, hard-boiled eggs, pickles, fresh fruit, cookies, doughnuts, pie, coffee, milk, and iced tea. A typical daily shopping list consisted of 175 loaves of bread, 100 pounds of meat, 15 pounds of cheese, two quarts of peanut butter and other spreads, 45 pounds of coffee, 40 quarts of cream, 500 half-pint bottles of milk, and 24 dozen rolls.

Probably the greatest treats were the birthday cakes—20 of them on an average day, some 600 a month—which were distributed on the honor system. The cakes usually came with a chorus of "Happy Birthday." Birthday cakes became a well-known tradition, and the focus of favorite canteen stories. One serviceman wrote to the ladies that he had lied about his birthday so he could get a cake to share with his buddies. His conscience bothered him so much that he gave the cake to a child with polio on the train! North Platte children frequently took their own birthday cakes to the canteen.

Not everyone could get off the trains. As the war ground on, more and more trains carried wounded to hospitals. The military gave the platform girls—they had to be at least sixteen years old—permission to take their baskets of goodies onto the trains to serve those who couldn't leave. The platform girls answered thousands of questions about North Platte, became adept at reeling off the distance between cities on either coast.

One unexpected by-product was terrific public relations for the little community. When the war ended, a significant number of returning GIs, impressed by the generosity shown them in those ten-minute bursts, opted to settle in the little town on the prairie.

The canteen closed on April 1, 1946, eight months after the end of the war. With changes in transportation patterns, the Union Pacific Depot closed in 1971, and was demolished a few years later. Today, a small park stands where it was located, with plaques honoring the townsfolk who took America's sons and daughters into its arms and nurtured them on the way to war.

This same spirit is alive and well today. I see it everywhere in America. The only New Year's Resolution I'm going to make this year has just one word: *Others*.

MARCH 17, 2005

THE COLOR OF FREEDOM? PURPLE AND GREEN

Color freedom purple. January's elections in Iraq had many of us feeling a little choked up. Last November when I voted, no one shot at me, and I didn't have to watch out for car bombers on 8th Avenue SW. I got a flag sticker for my troubles. No big deal.

It humbled me to watch the Iraqi election unfold and see people walking to the polls in family groups, not knowing if a terrorist was going to shoot them down or blow them up. They went anyway. Even just a whiff of democracy can do that to you.

When they finished, they displayed a purple finger, indicating that yes indeedy, they had cast a ballot. Some of them danced in the streets, and then they proudly walked home. There was nothing safe about what they did, but they did it anyway.

I was especially touched by those who took along their kids. When your children watch you do something brave, chances are they'll want to do it, too. I call that excellent parenting.

Thinking about those purple fingers, I remembered Leena Dawson and her green finger.

Leena's maiden name was Herlevi, and she's from Finland. When we were both a lot younger, we used to go running every morning. Leena and I always had a lot to talk about while we ran. Leena was raised in Finland and she remembers World War II. She also remembers the war before that, called the Russo-Finnish War, or the Winter War. Her mother, a math teacher, flew as a navigator on Finnish bombers.

Brief history lesson: The Soviet Union invaded Finland in 1939, pitting one million troops against an army of 175,000. They planned to chew off a chunk of the Karelian Isthmus, for whatever reason bullies think they need someone else's stuff.

Silly Soviets. They should have known better than to mess with people so famous for their *sisu*. (Translation: guts.) Until the Iraqis and their purple fingers, I used to think that Finns had the option on *sisu*.

Finnish men and women fought back with their customary ferocity. Those were desperate times. The government urged its citizens to donate money, silverware, heirlooms, and jewels, anything that could be converted into cash to buy war materiel. Like most Finns, the Herlevis gave all they had to resist the Soviet army. Leena likes to buy jewelry today, and I think part of her interest traces to the fact that her prosperous family gave up their gold in 1939.

Finland lost the war eventually, and the Soviets took that bite out of their country. Then the Really Big War got bigger, and the Russo-Finnish conflict faded into the background.

The Finnish government never forgot about the sacrifice of its citizen-soldiers. When World War II ended in 1945, the government wanted to show its gratitude to those who gave up their precious heirlooms and their wealth in defense of their homeland. But what could they do? The government was broke. With not even a pot to pee in, how could they express their thanks for such devotion in a time of desperate national emergency?

Because they were Finns, and full of honor and courage, they did the best thing. Everyone who had donated family treasure received a brass ring as a token of appreciation.

A brass ring. When you wear a brass ring, it stains your finger green. There was no greater honor in postwar Finland than to wear a brass ring and sport a green finger.

I was over at Leena's house one night and she showed me her brass ring. "Try it on," she said.

I couldn't. I hadn't earned the right to wear that cheap little ring. I touched the ring, and then Leena put it away.

Some things must be earned. Freedom is a costly prize. Just ask four families in the 141st. Ask Finns with green fingers, or Iraqis with purple ones. Freedom never comes cheap, but ordinary folks will go to extraordinary lengths to obtain it and keep it.

All I have to do is walk over to Washington Elementary School and vote.

SEPTEMBER 22, 2005

THINK FAST; DO IT NOW

Sometimes you've gotta do what you've gotta do. For every grown-up who dithered while New Orleans seethed and flooded, there were youngsters who took charge.

Give a medal—no, a college scholarship in 12 years—to that first-grader who led five children younger than himself to safety. Ditto for the young man (I've heard his age ranging from 14 to 20) who, when adults stood around, commandeered a bus, filled it with desperate people, and drove to the Houston Astrodome.

It reminds me of another evacuation. This time it was from a war zone, and the zone was Mexico in 1912.

The Americans involved were Mormons who settled in the Mexican states of Chihuahua and Sonora in the 1880s. The settlements became known as the Colonies: three in the mountains and three strung out 18 miles from the US border to 100 miles into Chihuahua.

The early days were tough. Settlers ate bread and milk with a fork to save milk. Housewives passed around one bacon rind from house to house to use in greasing bread pans. After 30 years, they were successful farmers and stockmen. The Colonies became known for their purebred horses and apple orchards.

And that became part of the problem. When Mexico burst into flames in 1910 with uprisings against Porfirio Díaz's corrupt government, rebels from all sides (and *federales*, too) began to steal horses and raid homes for food. Pancho Villa was one of those rebels.

When I lived in Ogden, Utah, 25 years ago, I interviewed Ervin Jackson, who was born and raised in Colonia Dublán. Ervin told me of the time Villa and his rebels rode up to his house. Ervin's father rushed all the women in the family down to the cellar to hide.

Ervin was 12. He and his father and brothers calmly made pancakes for Villa and his rebels, laughing and joking with them while his mother and sisters hid right below the kitchen.

Harassment worsened; finally, it was too much. Hearing the Mormons had stockpiled weapons for their own defense, rebels surrounded Colonia Dublán, pointed cannon on flatcars at the community, and demanded the rifles.

Junius Romney, church leader there and ancestor of Massachusetts Governor Mitt Romney, surrendered his town on condition that women and children be allowed to leave on the next train.

They thought they would be returning soon, once order was restored. One woman who had just canned 100 quarts of blackberries had her husband hide them under the porch. She never saw house or blackberries again.

The last train out was a terrifying experience. Bandits robbed the women and threatened to kill the children if anyone left the train for water. It was a hot, thirsty, frightening trip to El Paso, Texas.

When the evacuees arrived in El Paso, they took up temporary quarters in a lumberyard, staying there several weeks until everyone was accounted for. They were destitute, having left everything behind in their rapid flight to the border. Ervin and his family had nothing.

The day after his family moved to the lumberyard, Ervin went into action. The boy walked to the Cut Price Grocery and asked for a job. The owner asked if he could drive a truck.

Ervin never blinked; he said yes and was hired. It was Friday, and he was to start on Monday. "I'd never even been in a truck in my whole life," he told me, but Ervin knew he had to act decisively to help feed his family.

Ervin spent the weekend in El Paso's plaza. Every time he saw someone get into a car, he rushed over to watch. "I could see it was mostly a matter of footwork," he said. "When I went to work Monday morning, I killed the engine three times, but I got that truck to run."

I asked Ervin how he had the courage to do such a thing. After all, he was only a boy.

"I had to," he said simply.

Three cheers for kids—whether in Colonia Dublán or New Orleans—who aren't afraid of quick decisions. I know schools and parents work hard to bolster self-esteem. Some work equally hard to teach decision-making.

Adults in high places could take such a course. Maybe kids could teach it.

FEBRUARY 23, 2006

SOLDIERING ON WITH GUY HENRY

Guy V. Henry, US Army, was on my mind last week when the mercury hunkered down in the thermometer and I was whining about cold hands.

Henry died in 1899, but I know him well. I have a filing cabinet full of Guy Henry documents that I picked up on archives trips. I once presented a paper on him at an Indian Wars symposium. I will write his biography as soon as I find a wealthy patron to support me for a year. Anyone? Anyone?

In 1874, Captain Henry of Company D, Third Cavalry, was garrisoned at Camp Robinson (later Fort Robinson), located south of the Black Hills. One of the garrison's assignments was to keep miners away from the Hills. Gold had been discovered there that summer, but the area was off limits to everyone but Indians.

Right after Christmas, word came that miners had been spotted 105 miles north at Elk Creek. Henry was ordered to mount a patrol and apprehend them.

On December 26, Henry and 38 Company D troopers, plus 12 soldiers and their lieutenant of the Ninth Infantry, rode out. Before leaving, Henry borrowed officers' tents and stoves for his enlisted men.

Company D didn't find any miners. The company started back in early January, riding in weather that varied between -20 and -40 degrees. On January 8, 1875, the scouting detail found itself in a blizzard.

They couldn't go back; the wagons carrying the tents and stoves had taken a different route. They had no choice but to keep riding.

It was every leader's nightmare. The men dismounted and walked their horses because it was too cold to ride. Snow hid the trail. Many of the men couldn't see because of ice particles frozen on their faces and eyelids.

What do you do in a spot like that? In his official report of the incident that has gone down in Indian Wars lore as "The Black Hills Scout," Henry wrote simply, "An officer's duty is to save his men."

Henry knew his men and he knew horses. The patrol was lost, but he was sure it wasn't more than 15 miles to Camp Robinson. He ordered his men to mount, and tied the weakest into their saddles. He called "Forward gallop!" and ordered his men to turn it over to the horses.

Given their heads, the horses took their riders to shelter at a small ranch. Although he was in terrible shape, Henry saw his men inside, then rode—with assistance—to Camp Robinson, now that he had his bearings.

The next day, the quartermaster sent wagons to retrieve the men at the ranch. Everyone survived, with no amputations beyond some fingers and toes.

Henry suffered the most. When he came into his own quarters, his face was so swollen and black with frostbite that his wife, Julia, didn't recognize him.

The post surgeon had to cut away Henry's gloves, and the flesh came off, too. The first joint of one of his fingers was amputated, and he was never able to fully open or close his left hand again. (One pain for researchers: his handwriting is terrible.)

With all that was going on, Julia, seven months pregnant, went into labor and gave birth to their first son. They named him Guy Vernor Henry after his father. Guy Jr. scrawny at birth (and probably not looking a whole lot better than his father right then), grew up to serve the republic, too; like father, like son.

So here's to Guy Henry. What happened to him in the Black Hills Scout was a prelude to more pain and fame in 1876 at the Battle of the Rosebud, one week before the Little Bighorn.

Other famous battles and rides followed; Henry never hung back and neither did his troopers. After the Black Hills Scout, they knew their captain would get them out of any scrape or die trying.

When Henry was promoted to major and transferred to the Ninth Cavalry, the men of Company D gave him a hand-tooled saddle as a farewell gift. This was at a time when privates made $13 a month, and sergeants not much more.

Leadership is a gift, I think. I used to have a cat that followed me from room to room, but that's about it. Maybe I shouldn't whine so much about the cold.

MAY 25, 2006

SO MANY STORIES

Everyone has a story. I wish there was more time to write them.

Years ago, when we lived in Springfield, Missouri, I happened to run into Heine Bos in the mall.

Heine and I belonged to the same church, but we attended different congregations, so I didn't know him well. He was not one to beat around the bush, so our conversation was brief.

"I want you to write my life history," he said.

I get this a lot, but I knew I wanted to. Heine and Henne Bos were from the Netherlands. They had come to the United States after World War II, and I knew Heine had served in the Dutch underground during his country's Nazi occupation.

Earlier, he had told me one tantalizing story I have never forgotten. It's the only story I have, because Heine and I never got together.

I don't even know in which city this incident happened. I can hardly imagine a more dangerous enterprise than the underground, but there he was, a young man, hunted by the SS.

He had nowhere to hide, because to turn anywhere for help would only involve others and be their death sentence, too. He was running for his life, just a block ahead of the SS.

On nothing more than a whim, he ran to a house looking no different than any other house on the street. He banged on the door.

Henne opened the door. He told her, "Let me in. The SS are after me."

Without even thinking about it, Henne grabbed his arm and yanked him inside. She saved his life.

They were married a little later, the freedom fighter and a brave Dutch girl who had saved a stranger's life by not hesitating for one second. They raised a large family. Ironically, one of their daughters married a German.

That's all I know. Heine died a year or two after our conversation in the mall. Figuring I had plenty of time, I had never gotten back to him about writing his life story. I regret it to this day.

We left Springfield, moved to Louisiana for a few years, then returned. As the public relations coordinator for a four-state hospice, I was put in charge of Dr. Erich Loewy, medical ethicist, when he came to speak at a hospice conference.

Dr. Loewy is still alive. He's a small man; when I met him at the airport, he reminded me of a leprechaun: little and wizened, with amazing, lively eyes.

We got to talking, of course, and I learned that in addition to his medical ethics career, he is also a Holocaust scholar who lectures widely on the subject.

Erich was born in Vienna, Austria, to a prominent Jewish family. His father was a highly respected pediatrician.

This was 1930s Vienna, when things were going south quickly for the Jews. After the Anschluss, when the Nazis took over Austria, the Loewy family was suddenly not so popular. A young boy then, Erich observed firsthand how cruelly his distinguished father was treated.

Luckily, the family was able to flee Vienna and escape to the United States. There they remained, although all their European relatives perished in concentration camps.

Erich is a bit like Heine, not one to suffer fools. He has no patience with Holocaust deniers, who claim the deaths of six million Jews never took place.

For the skeptics, he has the perfect answer. He owns a prewar Viennese telephone directory, and he points out the thousands and thousands of Jewish names in it. He also has a postwar directory, which has no Jewish names.

"I ask the deniers, 'Where did these people go?'" he said. "The deniers can't tell me."

When I visited the Holocaust Museum in Washington, DC, in 2000, I thought of Erich Loewy and Heine Bos. In a museum crammed with one bludgeoning impact after another, the worst of all is the bridge over the river of shoes.

That's all it is. You cross a bridge and all around, where water would be, are shoes of all sizes—men's, women's, and children's: one pair for each dead person. Some are so small.

I stood there as long as I could, thinking about all the stories that would never be written, all the lives lost that no one remembered. It pained me then; it pains me now.

JULY 13, 2006

"THE CHAINS I FORGED..."

There's nothing lite about this column. The subject is death, or maybe something worse than death. Greed.

I've been thinking about the late Kenneth Lay, he of the Enron debacle, who, with his cohorts, looted and plundered shareholders and pensioners while at the same time pirating away his own fortune.

Maybe human nature dictates that more is better. Maybe the survival instinct dictates that even enough is never enough.

But it's not just humans. Animal behaviorists have studied greed in primates. In one experiment, scientists put a handful of candy in a jar with an opening just wide enough for a chimp's hand. The chimp immediately reached in and grabbed the candy.

Trouble was, once the chimp had the candy, that hand turned into a fist too large to get out of the jar. The scientists couldn't cajole that chimp to let go of some of the candy in order to get his hand out. The primate hung onto the whole lot, choosing to go hungry.

Greed can come back to bite you on the butt. Case in point—a fascinating memoir by Bernal Díaz del Castillo, who, as a young man, participated in the conquest of Mexico with Hernán Cortés in 1519–1520.

When he was much older, and a landowner in Guatemala, Díaz wrote his story of the conquest, one of the most vivid events ever. I don't know why this hasn't been made into a movie yet.

Cortes and some 450 Spaniards, many of them riding ferocious-looking armored horses, subdued the much larger Aztec civilization, but not without a big hiccup that nearly spelled disaster for them.

Mexico City—called Tenochtitlan then—was built on a series of islands in the middle of Lake Tezcoco. (Here's some geological trivia: Modern Mexico City, still on that spongy lake bottom, continues to sink.) To get to the city, Aztec engineers built causeways and bridges from the mainland to Tenochtitlan proper.

The Spaniards captured the city handily and proceeded to loot and pillage (refer to second paragraph). This irritated the good citizens of Tenochtitlan, who bided their time.

After numerous other blunders (refer to Iraq), Tenochtitlaners finally rose up and threw out the Spanish invaders. This is the most harrowing part of Díaz's memoir. I read it years ago in college and it remains vivid in my mind.

As many of the Spaniards retreated across the city toward the mainland, fighting every step of the way, the Aztecs pulled the bridges out of the causeways. It was sink or swim for the Spaniards.

Those who weren't weighed down with gold and silver loot made it to the mainland. The others who refused to abandon their swag drowned, killed by greed rather than arrows.

Gold trinkets. A silver bowl. How much is too much? If you have $10 million, must you have $30 million more? A billion or two? Who needs that much money? I remember a time when a ham on Easter would have made me happy. Would it now?

A jury of Lay's peers (seriously, who wants to be a peer of Ken Lay?) convicted him of milking a cash cow at the expense of an entire company. He wasn't the first and he won't be the last, because people are greedy.

Thousands lost their life savings and pensions when Enron collapsed, people who have every right to be bitter.

Many are. After Lay's sudden death, I read a series of online comments from people celebrating his death and lamenting that death meant he escaped justice, after all. The disappointment was mean-spirited but understandable.

Ironically, Lay's demise may result in throwing out his conviction, since he hadn't been sentenced yet. People with claims against his still-large estate may really go begging now.

Oh, well. Life is not a sure thing. People can rise fast and fall even faster. The dead are beyond our reach.

From Houston to Mexico to London, another image came to my mind, this one of Marley's ghost from Dickens's book *A Christmas Carol*.

The late Jacob Marley was Ebenezer Scrooge's partner in his London counting house. He comes back to warn Scrooge to shape up, or he's headed for eternity in an uncomfortable venue.

Marley is weighed down with chains. He laments to his former partner, "I wear the chains I forged in life."

Maybe it's time to rethink what we *really* need, before someone pulls a bridge out from under us.

NOVEMBER 16, 2006

I COULD DO THAT

"The line is busy."

Do you ever just want to smack that silly woman? Of course the line is busy. Just give me the busy tone. I don't want to hear one more computer-generated, snarky android telling me the line is busy.

Welcome to the 21st century; I wish it were a better fit. What I really wish is to look in the mirror and not see some old lady looking back.

I liked it better when planes flew lower in the sky, and I could hear them. I can't really explain why that was so neat, but it was. The drone of an airplane in a clear sky is one of the gifts of the gods.

I liked it better before polyester, when clothes were cotton. Mom would dampen the clothes slightly before she ironed them (remember ironing?). She would sprinkle them with water from a coke bottle that had a cork-based metal sprinkle top. I liked the smell of a hot iron on cotton, just this side of scorch.

I liked it better when we used to go on vacation. Dad leveled the backseat by putting suitcases down where our feet generally went, then covered it all with quilts. My sister, Karen, and I lolled around in the backseat, reading and eating little marshmallows.

Dangerous, you say? Probably. There wasn't a seat belt in sight. Nobody knew any better then, as we hurtled down the highway at 50 miles per hour. All I remember was the comfort.

I liked it better before chain restaurants. Each part of the country had its own specialties. After being exiled a couple of times in the East, I always knew when we were headed toward the Rocky Mountains because the breakfast plates featured hash browns instead of grits. If we were really lucky, there would be cowboys eating in the dining room, too.

It's entirely possible now to cross this country and eat the same food for every meal in a look-alike restaurant, but why would you ever do that? And I'm not sure where the cowboys went.

I always look for mom-and-pop eateries. A few years ago, I flew into San Antonio and my son Sam met me at the airport. We drove south on a non-interstate road, and outside of Floresville, there it was: a restaurant with a screen door and walls that hadn't seen a coat of paint since Travis died at the Alamo.

I ordered Sam to stop, and he humored me. We went inside, and sure enough, that was the best chicken-fried steak I had eaten since my last visit to Texas. (If you ever ask, "Carla, give me some advice," that would be it. "Only eat chicken-fried steak in south or west Texas. No exception.")

I liked it better when milk came in glass bottles and straws were made of paper. In fact, if you ask me, that's when the downfall of our civilization began: when straws went plastic.

I liked it better when kids read books, played outside, and weren't heavily scheduled. I remember Brownies and then Girl Scouts, and later on, music lessons, but that was it. When friends came calling, Karen and I were available.

I liked it better when we shared the roads in Wyoming with sheep or cattle, as stockmen trailed their livestock from one pasture to another. Karen got a camera one year and took a lot of photographs of cows' rear ends as we waited behind them for roads to clear.

A few years ago, I was traveling from Fort Union to Valley City. There was a cattle drive just off the road on Highway 83. If I'd had a camera, I'd have taken a photo of a cow's front, just to show Karen it can be done.

There are some things I don't miss. I'm glad the days of segregated bathrooms, and black folks sitting at the back of the bus, and chain gangs are over. I never liked seeing any of those things when I lived in Georgia because I knew it wasn't right.

I sometimes wonder if I'd like to go back to those earlier days in the '50s, when I was a kid. I think I might. Sure would be nice to drink a milkshake through a paper straw again. I could wear a cotton dress and sit with Karen at the lunch counter. I could do that.

AUGUST 9, 2007

OVERHEAD, UNDERFOOT

Forty years ago, when I was a sophomore at Brigham Young University, I took an art history class. During the semester, we studied the early Renaissance in England, which included looking at slides of King Henry VII's Lady Chapel in Westminster Abbey.

The chapel, dedicated to the Virgin Mary in 1519, has the most amazing fan-vaulted ceiling. There's nothing quite like it. The whole ceiling is covered with open fans: delicate tracery in stone. Amazing.

I decided in 1967 that someday I would stand under that ceiling. Few art objects have ever made me feel that way. I didn't know when, but I *knew* I would see that ceiling.

I saw it July 7. It was beautiful. I stood in the Lady Chapel, located at the east end of Westminster Abbey, and stared at the ceiling. Of course, the art and stonework on the walls was not exactly chopped liver, but oh, that ceiling.

Westminster Abbey is one huge sensory overload, containing the tombs of basically everybody who was anybody from monarchs to prime ministers, to soldiers, poets, painters, and musicians. It's a textbook come to life.

Queen Elizabeth I's tomb amused me, because she's stored in the same box with her sister, Queen Mary, who preceded her on the throne. Divided by religion (Mary was Catholic, Elizabeth was Protestant), the sisters didn't get along well. It must be a bummer to rub bony elbows for eternity with a barely tolerable sister. Too bad, ladies, and lots of luck. My sisters are far better.

At Poet's Corner in the south transept, the greats are buried—from Geoffrey Chaucer to Robert Browning and beyond—and others are memorialized. I patted Chaucer's coffin, made sure no one was listening, and thanked him for *Canterbury Tales*, still a good read after more than 600 years.

The Abbey, begun in the 11th century, was first a Catholic church. After King Henry VIII parted company with the Church of Rome, it became the Church of England's abbey. Every hour now, visitors are invited to join in prayer, led by a priest or chaplain.

One neat abbey moment involved a chaplain. I was standing in the nave by the dark wooden seats that line a good portion of the length, watching a young English family. The boy might have been 8, and his sister was younger. Their mother was telling them who might sit in those obviously important places.

A chaplain, moving fast and probably intent on getting somewhere, stopped to watch. He indicated one seat, not really any more distinguished than another, but located at the end of the row. He pointed to the word *decanus* carved on the wall behind the seat, and asked the boy if he knew whose chair that was.

The boy thought a moment. "The queen?"

He was right. His mother gave that my-boy-is-smart beam that's the same in any country. To everyone's delight, the deacon opened the wooden gateway and let the boy and his little sister sit in the queen's chair. Neat moment. I doubt the boy or his family will forget it; I know I won't.

The building was crammed with tourists from all over the world, but it was still possible, in that immensity, to have a private moment.

Mine came after I left the abbey itself and moved into one of the less-crowded corridors around the "cloister garth": a courtyard with grass that impossible shade of green which seems to be commonplace in the British Isles.

I was just walking along, looking into the courtyard, and then down at the paving stones underfoot, where people are both buried and memorialized. A large pavement stone had something like this engraved on it: "Here lie 29 monks who died of the plague in 1348."

I stood there a long time, thinking of the chaplain who had just charmed that boy and his family. Beneath me lay his hardworking brethren from a much earlier era who had probably prayed and worked (in St. Benedict's "Ora et labora" way) and died difficult deaths they couldn't have understood. They were Benedictines and used to spending themselves in service to others. Who helped them? How hard was it to die of the plague? What were their names? Does anyone remember them now but me?

Twenty-nine unknown monks. I went to Westminster Abbey for Henry VII's fan-vaulted ceiling; I'll remember the monks.

AUGUST 30, 2007

WHAT'S ON YOUR MIND?

I f I were asked to describe the neatest thing I saw in London, I think it would be the British Museum. It's old, it's huge, it contains basically everything in the world.

Everything except garbage cans—or bins, as the British say. It's hard to find garbage cans anywhere in London. This lack of places to park trash may date back to the time when the Irish Republican Army took a shine to blowing up prominent places and people. Garbage cans are handy places to park incendiary devices of one kind or other, so most public bins have been removed. I didn't see huge mounds of trash, so maybe the British do what we did—haul it around until you're back in your home or hotel.

I realize there are lots of great museums in the world. I've been to some of the biggies in the United States, but as far as I can tell, nothing tops the British Museum. You enter the Great Court, walk to just about the nearest exhibition room, and you're staring at the Rosetta Stone. I mean, there it is. That's hard to top. I'm no sophisticate—I had trouble wrapping my mind around the reality that I was actually looking at THE Rosetta Stone.

When the crowds get too big around that hunk of history, you walk a little farther and bingo! there are the Elgin Marbles. These are major portions of statuary and friezes taken from the Parthenon by British diplomat Lord Elgin—he said he paid the Ottoman rulers in Athens for them—and brought to England. In 1816, they came to the British Museum, and have remained there ever since.

Controversy swirls around those beautiful objects. Greece insists (and has insisted for years) they should be returned to Athens. Citing their excellent odds for continued preservation and safety in the British Museum, England wants to keep them. Other museums in other countries have bits and pieces of the Parthenon marbles, and some—not all—have repatriated them to Greece. Recent polls indicate that a majority of Brits would like to send the Elgin Marbles home to Athens, too.

I think they should stay where they are, even if the legality is a bit murky. Well, a lot murky. The Greeks might take good care of them, but there are way too many nuts jumping up and down and throwing tantrums in too many parts of the world right now. Just leave the priceless marbles alone, and rethink it some day when we're not taking off our shoes and removing body parts to get through airport screenings, or feeling downright discouraged when Taliban types blow up irreplaceable works of art in Afghanistan.

Maybe an even greater "museum" experience in London is a visit to Speakers' Corner at Hyde Park on a typical Sunday. Speakers' Corner is a living museum to free speech.

We showed up around 10:00 a.m., and the speakers were already in full voice. Anyone can join in. All you need is a box to stand on, or a step stool, and guts. You get on your soapbox and start talking. Pick a subject, any subject. One African-American with Muslim leanings had quite a crowd gathered around as he spoke at length on the superiority and ultimate domination of Islam. Most people listened respectfully. Some had questions, and others exchanged views.

Another speaker extolled—ahem—at length the virtues of that portion of anatomy that men have and women don't. A woman not far from him stood on a stepladder and declared us all evil sinners living in a vile world. I almost—but not quite—got up the nerve to ask her, "So what's your point?"

Maybe that's the point: She could say what she wanted, and her listeners were free to contradict, rebut, or agree. I didn't see any London bobbies ready to pounce or issue tickets. This was free speech at its finest, and also at its most bizarre.

In another corner was a man standing on a box and singing in Hebrew. Just a few feet from him were missionaries from The Church of Jesus Christ of Latter-day Saints, talking about the Book of Mormon. That's my church. I went up to them and wished them success.

I wish everyone success at Speakers' Corner. It's a little slice of living, breathing democracy in London. Say what you want there; it's your privilege and your right.

SEPTEMBER 20, 2007

YOU MUST REMEMBER THIS

I'm amazed by what people remember about their travels. When I worked at Fort Union Trading Post, I was in charge of the Elderhostel Program. For a week, Elderhostelers from all over the country came to Williston for history and visits to Indian reservations.

They left at the end of the week, except for one couple, whose flight was a day later. I volunteered to keep the fun going and drive Sandy, a physician, and his wife, a sculptor, down to the North Unit of Theodore Roosevelt National Park.

Sandy was astounded to see buffalo right on the road; the rock formations fascinated him. On the way back to Williston, he had me stop so he could pick some wheat. The harvest was over, but as you know, there's always wheat along the edge of the fields. I did what he asked, and he was so pleased. When he left the next day, he told me the North Unit was the neatest place he had ever seen.

I was stunned. It *is* a wonderful spot, but Sandy and his wife had traveled the world, and seen everything. That's the way it is with travel. Sure, you go for Westminster Abbey, the Tower of London, and the British Museum, but sometimes the small stuff lodges in the heart.

What could be smaller than a handful of Japanese schoolgirls? They were kindergarten age, and dressed alike in blue and white check dresses. Since July was near the end of the school year, we noticed many students on field trips. These little ones were touring St. Paul's Cathedral during our visit to London.

In the floor of St. Paul's are several circular, filigreed metal grids that allow observation into the crypt below, where lots of folks are buried. The little girls all decided to kneel in a circle on one grid with their noses to the filigree and their rumps in the air as they spied on the people walking below.

I'd have given anything for a camera. It was the funniest sight, and ironic, too. Here we were, in a cathedral with one of the world's most majestic ceilings, and these little misses were peering down into the crypt. It still makes me smile.

I had my own gee whiz moment in St. Paul's, and it was in that crypt. I knew he was there, but there's something about actually *seeing* Admiral Lord Horatio Nelson's coffin.

Sandy would have understood. I'm a fan of the Battle of Trafalgar, where in 1805, a Royal Navy fleet led by Nelson defeated the combined fleets of Spain and France. Nelson was shot on the deck of his flagship, HMS *Victory*, by a French sniper. He died below deck three hours later, but not before he knew the British had won. This victory confirmed Britain's mastery of the oceans.

There was Nelson's sarcophagus in the crypt, set on a high pedestal. Because Nelson was Nelson, he was not buried at sea. Typically, a ship's captain would be buried in his sleeping cot, which was literally a coffin. When in use, the sleeping cot would be slung like a hammock from the deck beams. When a captain died at sea, he was put in his sleeping cot, along with cannonballs for weight, and a lid would be tapped on. The whole thing went over the side of the ship. Buh-bye.

Not Nelson. Because he was a small man; his body was put in a keg filled with French brandy. There rose a rumor that on the voyage from the southwest corner of Spain to London, the crew used macaroni "straws" to drink down the brandy preserving him. The naval expression "tapping the admiral" (drinking on the sly) comes from that supposed event.

He was buried in a coffin made from the mast of *L'Orient*, one of the ships that took part in his other great victory, the 1798 Battle of the Nile. The coffin went into a sepulchre built originally for Cardinal Wolsey but never used by him because the cardinal fell out of favor with Henry VIII. Britain's greatest naval hero moved in instead.

I stood in the crypt before Nelson's coffin for quite a while. Maybe those little Japanese schoolgirls were looking down on me through the grillwork. We probably all had a good time. When I think of Nelson (and I do), now I'll think of them, too. Small moment, big memory.

NOVEMBER 1, 2007

THE GHOSTS OF VERSAILLES

Halloween is over. We still have candy, which is never a good thing, considering that we buy too much of what we like (anything with chocolate) under the fiction that it will all go to trick-or-treaters. Now that's scary.

I'm not a fan of horror movies. Who in her right mind would wander around a deserted hospital? Go into a dark room and *then* turn on the lights? Get into a perfectly operational car when trying to escape? It won't start. Doesn't she know that?

What really scares me is Pakistan, an unstable country with the atomic bomb. I'm equally frightened of wildfire marching over a ridge and all I have is a garden hose.

There's something about the supernatural that gives us that "zero-at-the-bone" feeling Emily Dickinson mentioned in her poem about snakes. It's chilling, but we're intrigued.

In 1901, two English academics on holiday visited the gardens of Petit Trianon, near Versailles. This faux farmhouse had been built during the reign of Louis XVI for the entertainment of his wife, Marie Antoinette. She liked to dress as a milkmaid, go there, and pretend she was doing something useful.

As Anne Moberly and Eleanor Jourdain followed the paths in search of Petit Trianon, they sidestepped into history. They described the event in their book, *An Adventure*, published in 1911.

Moberly and Jourdain claimed to have walked into 1789, seeing people and things that could only have been there in those pre-Revolution days, when the king and queen of France still had their heads.

After feelings of oppression and gloom settled on them, the women insisted they saw a repulsive-looking man, several gardeners dressed in 18th century livery, and someone warning them they were going the wrong way.

They were English ladies of the stiff-upper-lip type, so they ignored the warning and continued to Petit Trianon. Here, Moberly said she saw a woman in old-fashioned clothing, sketching. Soon, a footman hurried up, telling them the entrance to Petit Trianon was around the building. They went around, and found themselves back in the twentieth century.

Later, Moberly saw a painting of Marie Antoinette and realized it was the women she saw. She described the woman to her friend, and discovered that the other teacher hadn't seen the queen. She had seen other things, though. They decided to record their own accounts of the experience at Petit Trianon, and discovered they had been visiting Versailles on the anniversary of the attack on the Tuileries in Paris in 1792, when the Swiss Guards protecting the king and queen had been slaughtered by the mob.

Moberly and Jourdain began to wonder if what they saw at Petit Trianon was Marie Antoinette's stored memory of better times. Further investigation unearthed the fact that the queen had indeed been at Petit Trianon in 1789, when word came that the Parisian mob was marching on Versailles, which "explained" the teachers' oppressive feelings.

Was it a hoax? Probably. Evidence suggests Moberly and Jourdain did research the whole event, and "bent" history, in their zeal for others to see what they thought they saw. Maybe it would have been more convincing if they hadn't embellished the event. Who's to say that sometimes there isn't a window left open for a glimpse into the past? Still, it's best to take Versailles with a grain of salt.

And yet for years, I've hung onto "The Day We Saw Angels," a story that appeared in *Guidepost Magazine* in 1963. The event described took place in the 1930s in Massachusetts, on a morning Ralph and Marion Harlow went for a walk.

As they walked, they became aware of muted voices coming from behind them at a speed more rapid than they were walking. They turned around, but couldn't see anyone. When they realized the sound was above them, they looked up to see "glorious, beautiful creatures."

Six young women dressed in white glided along, engaged in a conversation the couple could hear, but not really comprehend. Unaware of the Harlows, the six creatures floated past, until the conversation faded out and they disappeared.

That was all. Shaken, Ralph asked Marion to describe exactly what she saw. She did, and it clicked with his view. This story convinces me because it's so ordinary. What it suggests is there are forces around us we can't explain and shouldn't try to.

All the same, stay out of abandoned hospitals, OK?

NOVEMBER 15, 2007

THE MORE WE GET TOGETHER

Remember that little song: "The more we get together, together, together, the more we get together, the happier we'll be." It's not always true. Sometimes the inmates end up running the asylum.

I'm referring to the flap in Breckenridge, Minnesota, where the school board, in its infinite wisdom, decided not to give the interim school superintendent a permanent three-year contract. This is the same superintendent—brave man—who chastised board members earlier this year for illegal meetings and other boneheaded shenanigans. And he's the same one who worked so hard to make sure the $770 per pupil operating levy referendum passed a few weeks ago, giving the school district some sorely needed dollars.

From the article in the *Forum*, I gather that the 150 Breckenridge residents and voters who booed the board's decision were a tad upset, too. Oops. Maybe it's time for Breckenridge to call for a vote of confidence, like the House of Commons does.

I have an idea. Make the Breckenridge school board switch places with the Red River Valley Fair board. I figure it can't get any worse.

Ah, committees and boards. It's seldom easy, and this is not a new phenomenon. They've been frustrating folks for centuries.

My personal favorite quotation of all time comes from Hyrum Smith. Hyrum was the older brother of Joseph Smith, the founder of The Church of Jesus Christ of Latter-day Saints, my church. Hyrum wrote this: "I would rather go to hell than be [on] a committee."

Hyrum was not one for messing around with committees. Sometime before that comment, the Mormons had gathered in Kirtland, Ohio. The Lord had commanded them to build the church's first temple there, but not much was happening.

One day, Hyrum showed up on the doorstep of his friend, Reynolds

Cahoon, and handed him a shovel. The two of them went to the church's temple site and dug the foundation by themselves. The building moved along at a rapid pace after that. In fact, the sturdy structure still stands, a beautiful building on a good foundation.

General Stonewall Jackson knew how to handle committees. Before the Civil War, he taught at Virginia Military Institute and, I suppose, found himself on committees here and there. After one meeting that went on entirely too long, Jackson had his Zen moment: For the next meeting, he took all the chairs out of the room. Amazing how that solved the problem of long-winded, gasbag discussion.

I think Jackson was a more able administrator than teacher. One of the courses he taught was mathematics. Once, a student raised his hand to say he didn't understand some principle Jackson had just covered. To solve the problem, Jackson read the entire chapter again, but in a louder voice. He was a better general.

Sometimes, committees do really good work. Not far into America's own experiment in government, it became pretty obvious the Articles of Confederation—adopted in 1777—weren't working. Each little state was its own kingdom, with no sense of obligation to a central power, something any country needs, if it hopes to succeed. Under the Articles, Congress lacked the coercive power to collect taxes, or the power to regulate commerce.

That issue of commerce got a few of the new states together for a conference in Maryland in 1786, but not enough of the states attended to resolve anything. Still, the idea that something needed to be done wouldn't—couldn't—go away.

Congress called for a gathering in Philadelphia a year later for the sole purpose of revising the Articles of Confederation. Fifty-five men assembled there in 1787. Thomas Jefferson—in Europe at the time—later called them demigods.

Indeed they were. Once gathered, they elected General George Washington to preside. The delegates were informed that the real purpose of the get-together was to scrap the Articles and start over. The firebrands of the revolution—Jefferson, John Adams, John Hancock, Patrick Henry—were not there. They weren't needed this time. Setting up a government requires reason and cold logic, not passion.

There were arguments, of course; much was at stake. Their job was made simpler because they were forbidden to discuss each day's doings outside of the assembly hall, and they weren't dogged by 24/7 newscasters, reporters, or paparazzi.

The result was the world's first and shortest Constitution. A committee never did better work. Thanks, guys. I'll be thinking of you when I eat turkey next week.

NOVEMBER 29, 2007

ERNEST GREEN AND MOM

Ernest Green is my hero; so is my mother, Dorothy Baier. Green was one of the Little Rock Nine, that handful of African-American students who integrated Central High School in Little Rock, Arkansas, on September 23, 1957. This year marks the 50th anniversary of the event. I don't know if local schools have included it in this fall's curriculum, but there's time.

Green was the only senior among the nine, which gave him a higher profile. It fell to Green to "prove" to America that a black kid could graduate from an all-white high school.

The action began a couple of years earlier, with the US Supreme Court's *Brown v. Board of Education* ruling that separate did not mean equal. Jim Crow laws in the South and elsewhere had led to second and third-tier everything for blacks in all aspects of life, from schools to movie theatres to lunch counters.

Green, a student at an all-black school, volunteered to be part of that brave little group to do what no students had done before: attend an all-white school in the South.

It seems like such a small thing today; it was not, in 1957. Green wrote that he was aware of *Brown v. Board of Education* and knew that the greater selection of courses, science labs, and library books at CHS was "an enhancement for my own personal education."

So he went with the other eight students, escorted into CHS by paratroopers from the 101st Airborne. Green said the first few weeks were tolerable, mainly because the hard-core pinheads stayed away from school. Gradually, though, they filtered back to class, and harassment and intimidation increased. The few whites who had earlier started to make friends were targeted, too, so that support vanished.

Talk about a tough year. Green said their lockers were constantly broken into, even when they were in "secret" locations. The Nine learned to carry everything with them. Green's physics teacher was openly antagonistic, and he struggled. The NAACP arranged for a tutor, though, no less a person than a white biophysicist from the University of Arkansas.

Graduation posed its own dangers. Some feared his participation would cause trouble, and Green was threatened. As he wrote, "I was laser focused on going because of the toil and tribulations we went through that year." When he walked across the stage—one of 600 graduates—only Green's family applauded. The family guest did, too: The Reverend Martin Luther King.

Green went on to Michigan State University on a scholarship from an anonymous donor and earned two degrees. Green is currently a senior managing director of public finance for Lehman Brothers, a global investment-banking firm. In 1999, he and others from the Little Rock Nine were awarded the Congressional Medal of Honor by President Bill Clinton. Few have deserved it more. Thank you, Ernest Green.

And thank you, Mom. In 1956, my mother attended a parent-teacher association meeting at St. Simons Elementary School on St. Simons Island, Georgia. She came home hopping mad after that meeting, telling us that everyone stood up and sang "Dixie" when the meeting started. (I think the standing up irritated her even more than the song.)

We teased her, and asked her if she stood up, too. "I did not!" she said, biting off each word. (I can still hear it.) I remember how indignant she was, even though she must have known we were yanking her chain. We knew she would never have stood up, and she didn't disappoint us.

That took guts. It's no fun to be the only person either standing up or sitting down, is it? Mom had some practice with courage, though. In 1944, she participated in an experiment in the US Navy. She was one of the earliest groups of WAVES—females in the wartime Navy—who elected to go to gunnery school.

She volunteered to join an experimental class training bombardiers to use the super-secret Norden Bombsight. The Navy wanted to know if women were smart enough to learn and train the men who would go overseas.

Mom graduated number one in the class, causing some hard feelings among her male classmates. She was part of a group of women who did equally well. Mom won the coin toss, so she became the first woman to drop a bomb from a US Navy plane.

Thanks, Mom. You're struggling right now with memory loss, so I'll remember for you.

DECEMBER 13, 2007

POINT A TO POINT B

This is a Christmas column. I'll get around to it eventually. You know me by now.

This summer, standing in the crypt in St. Paul's Cathedral and looking up at Admiral Horatio Nelson's coffin, I was struck again by the notion that considering our upbringing, who knows where in the world we'll end up? Nelson's life began in a country parsonage in rural England. It ended in 1805 aboard his flagship, HMS *Victory*, off the coast of Portugal, in the Battle of Trafalgar.

The victory of the Royal Navy there kept England free from Napoleon's conquest. Great Britain has never taken that effort lightly. Even today, Nelson ranks one or two in the distinguished list of England's heroes. His flagship, a floating museum, remains commissioned in the Royal Navy in Portsmouth Harbor.

John Paul Jones lies today in an equally elegant crypt at Annapolis, home of the US Naval Academy. Son of a gardener, he started life on an estate near Kirkcudbright, Scotland. He took to the sea to an early age, as many did from that lovely southwest Scottish coast, working on and later commanding merchant vessels trading with the American colonies and British holdings in the Caribbean.

After a colorful and somewhat controversial career there, he eventually ended up in the colony of Virginia, where his brother had property. Never content away from the sea, he gravitated to naval warfare when the American Revolution began. Jones spent several years on the USS *Ranger*, terrorizing British shipping lanes, and eventually took the fight to England as captain of the USS *Bonhomme Richard*. His 1779 battle with the HMS *Serapis* off the Yorkshire coast is the stuff of legend.

Jones was never good with politicians, and he was a restless soul. By 1788, he was a rear admiral in the Russian Navy, where he distinguished himself, but ran afoul of jealous underlings. He ended up in revolutionary Paris, where he died in 1790.

His body was later identified and transported to the US, where as Father of the US Navy, he was reinterred at the Naval Academy. Not bad for a gardener's son from Scotland, but a long way from home.

This brings me to Barbara Johnson. When I met her years ago, she was a secretary in the radiology department at St. Benedict's Hospital in Ogden, Utah. I worked in the public information department.

I wrote the hospital newsletter and asked readers to submit Christmas stories. Barbara did, and hers remains my favorite. In her story, Barbara described childhood Christmases in Germany before World War II, and how she and her siblings would try to stay up late to see Kristkindl, the Christ Child.

Her story turned next to Christmas in Bremerhaven, Germany, in the last winter of World War II. Barely out of her teens, Barbara was a secretary in a naval hospital. Before Christmas, the secretaries were ordered to go into the wards, to serve as nurses.

She had no nurse's training, but the hospital was desperate. Working with nothing, she and the other secretaries did what they could to relieve suffering.

In the middle of all that agony on Christmas Eve, someone found a pine branch and stuck it in a fire bucket filled with sand. They took it to one of the wards, and that was Christmas. That night, one of the wounded soldiers started singing "Stille Nacht." Everyone who could sing joined in. This was a far cry from the Christmases of Barbara's youth, but it was the one she remembered best, because for just a moment, all was calm, all was bright.

By spring, the situation was hopeless. Barbara and others were released and told to go home. In her case, this was Berlin. She was there during the terrible days when the Russians conquered the city and were particularly cruel to its women.

"Rough?" I asked her.

She nodded; I didn't press the issue.

Barbara got lucky. She met a GI from Utah on occupation duty in Berlin and came to America. They married and raised a family. When I met Barbara, she was a grandmother and nearing retirement.

It's been years since I've seen Barbara. I've never forgotten her story of the Christ Child of her youth, and the Kristkindl in battle-weary Bremerhaven. She's a long way from home, but her story of Christmas and the peace it can bring—even in a desperate hospital—echoes everywhere.

DECEMBER 20, 2007

THE RODEO QUEEN

We met Mary Lynn Chino in Ogden, Utah. She always wanted to be a rodeo queen. Mary Lynn was OK-looking, but no rodeo queen and not young either. I'm not even sure she knew how to sit on a horse. It happened to be one of those childhood fantasies that never morphed into reality.

I remember laughing with her about beauty pageants, and those starry-eyed chicks who tell the emcee they want world peace.

They're right, though. World peace wouldn't be a bad idea; not at all. My apologies, ladies. What you're wishing for is the best idea of all time.

If you were to ask them, I think my children's favorite Christmas story is one about Gail Halvorsen, a US Air Force pilot during the Berlin Airlift in 1948. We came across it in the *Deseret News*, and it found a place in our collection of stories we read during the Christmas season, when the Kelly kids were growing up.

Halvorsen piloted a C-54 cargo plane—one of many transporting food, coal, everything—to blockaded West Berlin, which was surrounded by Soviet troops eager to swallow up the still-democratic part of the city. Around the clock for more than 18 months, cargo planes landed every 90 seconds at Tempelhof Airport, as the free world remained determined to deny West Berlin to communism.

Berlin was a city of two million people, so the task was nearly impossible. Still, West Berliners endured starvation and deprivation to remain democratic.

The Airlift was grinding, but Halvorsen took a few moments once to sightsee around Tempelhof, where he noticed a group of ragged kids watching the city's lifelines land, disgorge supplies, and take off. Halvorsen approached the group and tried out his halting German. Some kids knew a little English, so he spent a few moments chatting and unable to overlook their starving condition.

As he left, he was struck by the fact that no one had asked him for anything. He knew that in other areas, kids gathered around GIs for gum and chocolate. Not these children; they were too defeated. Halvorsen checked his pockets and found only two sticks of gum, which he broke into tiny pieces and handed out as far as they would go. The kids who didn't get any were still overjoyed to smell the wrappers.

Disturbed, Halvorsen decided to do what he could on his next flight over Berlin. He got some candy, tied it to three pocket-handkerchief parachutes, and he dropped them out of his flare tube on the approach to Tempelhof. He also wiggled his plane's wings so the kids would know it was the Candy Bomber.

Word got out. Halvorsen was afraid his commanding officer would be upset, but he wasn't. Instead, the general saw the morale potential for Berlin. Journalists dubbed Halverson "Uncle Wiggly Wings." By Christmas, Halvorsen and fellow pilots had dropped some 90,000 candy parachutes over Berlin.

It was called Operation Little Vittles. Candy came from all over the United States. Eventually, 6,500 pounds of candy—too much for the flare tubes—was landed at Tempelhof and distributed at Christmas parties for children throughout the city.

In all, more than 23 tons of candy was dropped from cargo planes for the children. Berliners never forgot. Years later, when Halvorsen returned to West Berlin as base commander at Tempelhof, he was greeted as a national hero. A school was named after him. The US Air Force has named a transport plane for him, and an air transport award.

Germans still remember. During the 2002 Winter Olympics in Salt Lake City, Halvorsen, a spry 82, carried the German team's placard into the Olympic stadium.

I like Halvorsen's words better than mine. He had to fly on Christmas Eve in 1948 to Berlin, which went into blackout mode at nightfall:

"As I left the West German base for the last of my 450-mile round trips that night, fireworks exploded around me. But in West Berlin, there was only darkness. On Christmas Eve, it was eerie.

"*What a people!* I thought. Surrounded as they were, an island in an ocean of Russian troops, they fought on, living on half-rations. Just weeks before, during a general election, 99 out of 100 West Berliners had voted dramatically against acceptance of Communism. How could I be anything but grateful for having known these people?"

That was 1948. Sixty years later, world peace still can't come a minute too soon. Beauty queens of the world, thanks for the occasional reminder. We need it.

MARCH 26, 2007

IMAGES BURNED ON THE RETINA

While in San Diego recently, I went to an exhibit called "A Day in Pompeii," presented at the Museum of Natural History in magnificent Balboa Park. Those of us old enough to have studied history when it meant something have a good idea which day: August 24, AD 79, when Pompeii vanished under lava. In less than 24 hours, the prosperous seaport town on the Bay of Naples vanished when Mt. Vesuvius blew its top.

Using good flow, audio information, and well-chosen artifacts and images, the exhibit told the story of a truly trying day, worse than ones when you burn dinner, the laundry comes out pink, or your kid tells you at bedtime that he needs two dozen cupcakes tomorrow, first thing.

Featured artifacts included carbonized olives, bread, and other foodstuffs, gold jewelry, medical probes and scalpels, dinnerware, statues, and coins. Most astounding were what we probably all came for: eight plaster casts of the dead.

When Pompeii died and was buried under an immense lava flow, the people who perished remained in place, as the city was largely forgotten. Entombed in lava, their bodies decayed down to bones or even less, leaving a human-shaped cavity in the hardened material around them. In 1860, an Italian archeologist cleverly poured plaster into the cavities, let it set, then knocked away the lava.

What remained has a high gulp factor. The human forms are complete, right down to understandably grim expressions as people ran, sat, or cowered, choked on the ash and intense heat and died. This is not a good way to die, but it probably was quick. Some 1,500 such casts have been made; the San Diego exhibit had eight.

The most touching ones are of a couple. She is lying on her back, and he is trying to cover her face. His dying efforts on her behalf were puny and wholly inadequate, obviously, but it said a lot about that particular couple, whoever they were. I wonder what they said to each other as they lay dying. Who *were* these people?

The exhibit got me thinking about two photos that, through the years, have chilled me to the bone. The first image shows an anonymous Frenchman sobbing after the fall of France in June 1940. He's in his forties, well-dressed and crying at the photographer as German *soldaten* goose-step down the Champs Elysees.

An unforgettable image of utter despair, the Frenchman has a rival in another photo that is also burned on my retina. On May 20, 1948, the Three Affiliated Tribes of Fort Berthold were forced to sell 155,000 acres of Missouri River bottomland to the federal government. The photo shows George Gillette, tribal chairman at Fort Berthold Reservation, as Secretary of the Interior J. A. Krug signs the document for the construction of the Garrison Dam and subsequent creation of what would become Lake Sakakawea.

In tears, Gillette has covered his face with his hand and turned away. Looking utterly complacent next to Gillette's agony, Krug signs the document that was supposed to bring Progress with a capital P to North Dakota, and probably provide the state's residents with just about everything from lemon meringue pie to chartreuse Cadillacs.

Money changed hands and there were promises aplenty to the Three Tribes. The tribes had a hospital at Elbowoods, one of several little towns which slowly sank as Lake Sakakawea rose. The tribes were promised another hospital, but there's still no hospital to replace the one that disappeared in 1953. Water quality is not so good on the reservation, either; neither is access. The lake effectively cut the reservation into pieces, so it's hard to get around, especially if you're old, or ill, or lacking in resources.

The irony now is that Lake Sakakawea is drying up, much like those promises already have. As the lake sinks, maybe the reservation will get its land back, as the Missouri River returns to its age-old bed. Maybe residents will finally get a hospital in New Town; maybe pigs will fly.

Speaking of pigs: In addition to the body casts, the Pompeii exhibit also has a plaster pig wearing a startled expression. The pig is in San Diego until June, when the exhibit travels to North Carolina, last stop on the journey home to Italy. From 79 to 2008, that pig has accumulated considerable mileage. But as someone says in the musical *Big River*, "What's time to a pig?"

APRIL 3, 2007

LONG TIME, NO SEE

I broke a North Dakota rule this winter: Never read about cold during a cold winter. I read *Frozen in Time*, an account of the Franklin Expedition of 1845–48 sent to find and map the Northwest Passage.

The Franklin expedition came to my attention years ago, when I watched a documentary about the Royal Navy's attempts to explore islands near the Arctic Circle and find the fabled Northwest Passage. In the nineteenth century, Great Britain spread its influence globally until nothing was left to explore except the frozen north. Supremely confident, the navy planned to fill in the last blank spots on the map.

There's no more bleak place in the world than the islands of northern Canada. Few go there. In the 1840s, Inuits sometimes passed through the area in summer, but no one stayed. It was too inhospitable. Inuits were not then, and are not now, foolish.

Into this region came the ships, well provisioned for a three-year expedition to a place everyone else had the good sense to avoid. Entering from the east, Sir John's task was to complete a mapping of the region begun earlier, and exit in the west, into the Bering Strait.

The expedition utilized a new technology: canned food. The ships carried 8,000 tins of canned goods, plenty for a three-year exploration. By the 1840s, everyone knew that lime and lemon juice would prevent scurvy, that dreadful and often-fatal disease of the deepwater sailor. The expedition had taken that into account, too. No detail was too small to escape notice.

What no one anticipated were colder than normal summers in the region. The *Terror* and the *Erebus* sailed into Lancaster Sound in 1845 and vanished. By 1847, the ships still hadn't popped out of that western end. Where were they?

In years to come, several expeditions were mounted to find Franklin and his 128 men. The rescue expeditions proved as dangerous as the initial voyage. Gradually, the story came out—how the ships were finally trapped and choked in pack ice, with what remained of the crew forced ashore, where they suffered and died. Some tried to travel south to a Hudson's Bay Company post 2,000 miles away, nothing but a forlorn attempt by desperate, starving men. The shocking deaths involved cannibalism, madness, and probably enough despair to circle the earth two or three times.

In recent years, Canadian scientists took an interest in the sad story. Mounds of empty tin cans from the Franklin Expedition had been found, giving testimony to the highly probable cause of death by lead poisoning. Researchers discovered that the primitive cans were soldered in a way that allowed the lead to seep inside. Add that to scurvy, and the sailors probably never knew what hit them.

In the early 1980s, anthropologist Owen Beattie of the University of Alberta led a team of scientists to tiny Beechy Island, where three graves of Franklin Expedition members had been located years earlier. Beattie received permission to exhume the bodies of two sailors and one Royal Marine who died in that first winter of 1846, when things weren't desperate yet. Beattie needed tissue samples to test for lead content.

Over the course of several summers, Beattie and his scientists dug up those crew members, X-rayed and autopsied them right there on Beechy Island. Because they were buried below the permafrost, the corpses were in astoundingly good condition.

Here's what struck me about the whole experience. Here's what I can't forget. One of Beattie's scientists was Brian Spenceley, a great-great-nephew of John Hartnell, who died Jan. 4, 1846, and was buried on Beechy Island.

When the scientists opened Hartnell's coffin for the first time in 140 years, Spenceley looked on the body—not the skeleton—of a long-dead uncle. Hartnell's eyes were half open. In the photographs, he looked not quite alive, but not quite dead.

Beattie described the emotional experience of studying the bodies, and the extreme reverence the team used in its scientific work. When the scientists finished, the bodies were reburied carefully. Everything was replaced the way it had been, before anyone interrupted the men's long sleep on Beechy Island.

And there was Brian Spenceley, with a story no one else in the world could tell. On Beechy Island, he had the awesome privilege of gazing at someone no one else has ever seen: a truly distant relative from another era. *Frozen in Time* is a hard book to forget.

APRIL 17, 2008

AS WE WERE SAYING YESTERDAY

In the 16th century at the University of Salamanca, Father Luis de Leon was teaching his usual class in theology one day. (There were probably students dozing on the back row, but at least no one was wasting time on a laptop.) Father de Leon had come to the attention (and how) of the Spanish Inquisition because he had the nerve to translate the Bible into Spanish, or so the story goes.

Smack dab in the middle of his lecture, goons from the Inquisition stormed into his classroom and hauled him away, doing a 16th century version of the "perp walk" so beloved of—oops—Eliot Spitzer, when he was the cop of Wall Street.

De Leon languished in prison for five years before his release. When he got out of the slammer, he returned immediately to his classroom and began his lecture with the words, "Como decíamos ayer," which translates literally to, "As we were saying yesterday." In the Spanish world at least, that phrase became a cry of defiance to anyone thinking a mere prison term could squash a good idea whose time had come.

Incidentally, there is a plaque with those words on it outside the door of de Leon's classroom, which, after nearly 500 years, is still a classroom. There is also a statue of de Leon in the courtyard of the U of Salamanca. Take that, Inquisition.

I first heard this story from Dr. George Addy, a professor at Brigham Young University, when I took Spanish history from him. Addy had attended the University of Salamanca himself, while working on his doctorate. Through the years, I've used the phrase occasionally, when it was appropriate. I've wanted to use it here in Valley City, but I never was sure anyone would get it. Sometimes "Como decíamos ayer" is the only response. Well, now you know.

I was reminded of this recently when I read a lovely editorial by Sean

Connery, a Scot probably better known as James Bond: Mr. Shaken, Not Stirred himself. Connery wrote of today's growing independence movement in Scotland, which, in 1707, was sold out by Scottish traitors to the English crown and subjugated. That nation of oatmeal, haggis, grim Calvinism, and cold knees became a fiefdom of Great Britain and remained so until 1997, when the people of Scotland voted to restore their own parliament.

Connery wrote movingly of that first parliamentary session in 1997, when Scottish National Party President Winifred Ewing had her own *como decíamos ayer* moment. She opened Parliament by saying, "The Scots Parliament, adjourned on 25th March 1707, is hereby reconvened." I doubt there was a dry eye in the hall. I know I felt the same way when I read Connery's column, and my ancestors left Kirkcudbrightshire in 1867.

Currently, the Scottish parliament legislates only in matters of health (why on earth hasn't some lawmaker banned fried Mars Bars?), education, courts, and the environment. Matters of taxation and foreign affairs continue to reside with Britain's Parliament.

But the sentiment for full independence is there and growing. When I was in Edinburgh last summer, I noticed "It's Scotland, not England," scrawled on more than one building. A journalist until I die probably, I asked several Scots how they felt about full independence. The consensus was a cautious yes, cautious because Scotland is not a wealthy nation, and there would be belt-tightening when British social benefits leave town. Scots are no fools.

But many do want full independence. According to Connery, polls indicate that two-thirds of Scotland's people are in favor. I think it will happen, and I hope independence comes in my lifetime. It'll be a peaceful separation, unlike our own revolution. Scots are ferocious in battle, but they are still no fools, and times have changed.

There will be details to iron out. As I wrote in an earlier column, Scotland has already reclaimed the Stone of Scone, which plays a significant role in the coronation of a British monarch. The Stone will be loaned to Great Britain when the next king is crowned in Westminster Abbey, then returned to its proud spot in Edinburgh's Castle among Scotland's crown jewels.

Of course, when Scotland eventually becomes independent, that Stone ain't going nowhere ever again, because there will be no united Scotland and England. As Father de Leon understood, and as Scotland also knows, good ideas are almost impossible to squelch forever.

MAY 22, 2007

VOTE FOR THE PAST

With the possible exception of writing, I'm not a forceful person. I seldom make demands on anyone, but I'm asking you on June 10 to vote for the proposed 12 mil levy increase for Barnes County's museums.

As Allen Siebert pointed out in his excellent letter to the editor this week, that's only $2.25 a year on a house or other property of real value of $100,000. The additional $18,000 a year would be divided between Barnes County Historical Museum and the museums in Wimbledon and Litchville. Sounds like a bargain to me.

I love museums, from the Range Riders Museum in Miles City, Montana, with that doughnut made during the Battle of Gettysburg, to the British Museum with its Rosetta Stone. I worked in and around museums during my years with the National Park Service. Heavens, when we rangers did Living History, I *was* a museum. I used to almost pinch myself on payday, when I realized I was getting paid to be a caretaker of my country's past. What an honor; I'd have done it for free.

When I was lucky enough to teach American history at two universities, I really took seriously the sections on the American Revolution, the Constitution, and those early Supreme Court cases that defined our magnificent nation. It mattered to me, and I wanted it to matter to every student I taught.

I fear that people who never learn about their country's past, or disregard it as a waste of time, have less respect for it. Some tend not to vote, because there can be a disconnect between knowing where we came from and understanding what it takes to keep our liberties. Early settlers in Barnes County, many from Scandinavia and Germany, understood this perfectly well. Their children were schooled in American history and values because their parents knew they mattered.

Museums preserve these values. Even that quirky Civil War doughnut in Miles City tells us something about the people of Gettysburg. Some hid in cellars as the war's turning point raged in their quiet college town. Others made doughnuts for the soldiers. With its three languages, the Rosetta Stone represents a milestone in the understanding of previously "lost" languages. A punched ration card in the Museum of the American Indian speaks volumes about the disrupted lives of people, now dependent on flour and sugar rations, who once roamed the plains and lived on buffalo. Warts and all, it's our history.

I enjoyed the article in Monday's *Forum* about fifth graders from Bennett Elementary School who tested West Acres Mall shoppers' knowledge on the US Constitution. According to the article, some shoppers were clueless, others embarrassed. I hope some got the answers right.

Personally, I would have argued with the answer to Question D: *What right is given in the 15th Amendment of the US Constitution?* The answer given as correct was: "The right for people of all races to vote."

That's misleading. The 15th Amendment reads: "The rights of citizens of the United States to vote shall not be denied or abridged by the United States or by any State on account of race, color, or previous condition of servitude." A better answer to Question D would be, "The right for men of all races to vote."

Using the students' answer, some people who don't have a copy of the Constitution to refer to might conclude that women, who are indeed people, were included in the 15th Amendment. Not so. When this amendment was adopted in 1870, no women in America of any color or race had the right to vote. Female US citizens did not earn that right until 1920, when the 19th Amendment was adopted.

Had I been the teacher of Bennett's gifted and talented program that supervised the Constitution course, I'd have taken a moment to discuss just who the electorate was in 1870, and then maybe touch on the fact that as early as 1869, Wyoming Territory granted its female citizens unrestricted suffrage. Utah Territory followed in 1870, and then gradually most of the western states. Then we could speculate on why the western United States was so far ahead of the eastern half, voting rights. History, plus kids, plus questions add up to an informed electorate. This kind of questioning is food for the brain.

Please vote yes for that mil levy and support our museums. It has always amazed me—humbled me, too—that places devoted to the past foretell our future.

JUNE 26, 2007

WOULDN'T IT BE LOVERLY?

Does America have a new romantic hero in a space station astronaut? What's so nice is he declared his love for his wife so publicly and said something interesting about people and the nature of love.

I'm referring to Garrett Reisman, who recently returned to earth from a three-month assignment at the international space station. During a broadcast, the soon-to-leave astronaut was asked what he was looking forward to. Reisman had two words: "Simone Francis," his wife. He joked that he was bound for the doghouse by embarrassing her, but what he said next makes me think she was probably pleased:

"But the truth is that when I look out the window at the planet and I look down at all the people down there," he said, "I'm usually just thinking about one of all those billions of people. And that's definitely what I'm looking forward to seeing the most."

How true. Seen from space, Earth is a lovely planet with clouds and blue water. One of the principal reasons Earth is so beautiful in another way is because of those loved ones who inhabit the planet with us.

I seriously doubt Garrett Reisman remained in the doghouse long. What must it have been like for Simone Francis to look up and know that her husband was looking back at her? Love connects us, even though miles get in the way. I hope the Reismans had a happy reunion.

They got me thinking about lovers through the ages—not the famous or handsome ones, but couples whose expressed feelings have the power to remind us how enduring love is between two people, on this planet with so many people.

In Hollywood terms, Abigail and John Adams were nothing to get excited about. They loved each other through perilous times in our colonial and early republic era, when they were often separated because of war and duty. Here's part of a letter from Abigail to John, middle-aged fuddy-duddies, dated December 23, 1782:

"Dearest Friend, . . . should I draw you the picture of my Heart it would be what I hope you still would Love; tho it contained nothing new, the early possession you obtained there, and the absolute power you have maintained over it, leaves not the smallest place unoccupied." And this: ". . . nor have the dreary years of absence in the smallest degree effaced from my mind the Image of a dear . . . man to whom I gave my Heart."

I enjoyed this snippet from a letter Oliver Cromwell sent to his wife in 1650. It appealed to me particularly because some recent family history research I acquired has confirmed that the Cromwells are distant relatives of mine. Nice to know that even if Cromwell played a major role in seeing that King Charles I lost his head, he still had a sentimental side:

"My Dearest, Truly, if I love thee not too well, I think I err not on the other hand much. Thou art dearer to me than any creature; let that suffice. I rest thine, Oliver." Ah-hah! Cromwell also knew how to use a semicolon properly. Maybe I inherited his semicolon gene; perhaps he is a resident of Planet Grammaria already.

Sometimes letters from historical figures are best kept from young eyes. It's a dirty little secret of Indian Wars historians that the controversial Lieutenant Colonel William Benteen of the Seventh Cavalry decorated love letters to his wife with—ahem—little doodles of his manly anatomy. I had to smile when I read his letters and gaped at his drawings, considering how thoroughly they trashed notions of Victorian prudery. Fred was a rare old dog.

He knew how to conclude a letter: "Well, Wifey, Darling, I think this will do for a letter, so with oceans of love to you . . . and kisses innumerable, I am devotedly, your husband, Fred."

I like this comment from Jane Welsh to her future husband, Scottish essayist Thomas Carlyle: "When I read in your looks and words that you love me, I feel it in the deepest part of my soul; and then I care not one straw for the whole Universe beside . . ."

Ah, the universe, the one that astronaut Reisman traveled in as he thought of his wife. Among all the world's billions, we single out our few special people and cherish them for a moment here, then longer elsewhere, if we're lucky.

AUGUST 14, 2007

RORKE'S DRIFT

Our television crashed. The screen went violently orange, and then it just perished. I can't say this was unexpected. Martin had bought the thing 12 years ago secondhand, so we had no idea how old it really was—you know, kind of like a cat that wanders into your life and stays.

We thought we'd buy another set for a modest sum, which gives you some idea of when we last went television shopping. Now the only TVs available are those skinny guys with the big price tags. I gulped and bought one, mainly because we can't do without *Jeopardy*. (It's a family joke. Our kids know better than to phone during *Jeopardy*.)

The skinny television was duly installed, and one night last week, I channel-surfed. This eventually landed me on a movie channel, about an hour into *Zulu*. I was hooked; no matter that I have it on VHS—I had to watch.

If there was ever a more fraught battle than at Rorke's Drift, January 22–23, 1879, I've never heard of it. In Natal Province, South Africa, fewer than 90 British and South African soldiers—another 35 were ill—held off a force of more than 4,000 Zulu warriors and lived to tell about it. They weren't even defending a proper fort, but a church mission which had been temporarily turned into a supply depot. The men of the 24th Foot (later renamed the South Wales Borderers) were there to guard supplies, and nothing more.

Their leader was a mere lieutenant named Gonville Bromhead, age 33. He was superseded in command by another lieutenant, John Chard of the Royal Engineers, who had been sent there to build a bridge. All arguments of line versus staff aside, Chard probably assumed command because Bromhead was nearly deaf.

So there they were in the middle of nowhere. It was too late to run, because they had almost no warning. Earlier on the 22nd, the massive Zulu army had overwhelmed a British and native army force at nearby Isandhlwana, killing some 1,300 soldiers. Ironically, the greatest defeat of a British force in a single action, up to that time, was to be followed by its greatest lopsided victory at Rorke's Drift.

Eleven Victoria Crosses (think, Congressional Medal of Honor) were awarded to the defenders of Rorke's Drift for incredible heroism, plus five Distinguished Conduct Medals. Talk about well-earned medals.

Best book on the subject is Donald Morris's *The Washing of the Spears: The Rise and Fall of the Zulu Nation*. Written in 1959, it remains the gold standard on the Anglo-Zulu War. To the Zulu, washing a spear means to dip it in the blood of an enemy. I suppose it's like counting coup among the Plains Indians.

But hey, the movie is as good as the book. *Zulu* came out in 1964 and starred Stanley Baker as Chard, and Michael Caine as Bromhead. *Zulu* was filmed on location in Natal, not far from the actual mission, and featured more than 500 Zulu extras. Because of apartheid, the Zulu were not allowed to receive the same pay as the white extras in the movie. Director Cy Endfield got around that bit of stupidity by paying the Zulu their pittance, then giving them herds of cattle, which were much more valuable to them.

There are so many quotable lines in the film. You'd laugh if you joined a screening of *Zulu* with historians and reenactors, who would quote them all. My personal favorite is when one frightened soldier says to veteran Color Sergeant Frank Bourse: "Why us?" Imperturbable Bourse replies, "Because we're here, lad, and nobody else, just us."

A skeptic forever, I wonder how many of those great lines actually were said. Probably none; I don't care. We used to hash around stuff like this is graduate school, and someone would invariably comment, "Well, they should have said it."

Watching the film this time, I was in awe all over again at what ordinary, disciplined people can do when they have no choice. I was also struck by something else: There wasn't a CGI moment anywhere. All the hundreds of Zulus were real; every British soldier at the Drift was flesh and bone, and not digitized. I hope no one ever dares to remake *Zulu*. I won't see it. The washing of the spears using a green screen and a computer would be like giving the finger to bravery.

SEPTEMBER 16, 2007

TV JOURNALISTS AND THE GENE POOL

I've been accused of being easily entertained, but nothing gives me the giggles as much as television journalists reporting a hurricane. Watching earnest reporters being blown sideways or even out of camera range by a strong wind makes me laugh out loud and practically slap my knee, shouting, "Dadburn, that's rich!" In the first place, they look really silly; in the second place, these dipwads could be part of the problem.

I have a strong suspicion that these stupid hotshots drive law enforcement officials nuts, because maybe they're part of the reason people don't evacuate when they should. I mean, if Manly Newshound can hang onto a flagpole in Galveston and not be blown shoeless into Springfield, Missouri, then gee, maybe I can hunker down in my beachfront house while 100 m.p.h. winds barrel down, and survive. I watch TV journalists and think, "You're an idiot. Go ahead, blow away. Shrink the gene pool."

Those televised pre-storm efforts leave me shaking my head too, as I watch people go to stores for plywood and batteries. Hmm. If they've been through this a time or two and there is still a house standing, why not just save last year's plywood somewhere and reuse it?

Then I start asking myself—after Katrina, Rita, and now Ike—why not just move farther inland? Billings is nice. I understand a sense of fatalism does develop in areas that are often the target of Mother Nature. I mean, why else would millions of people live in or near Naples, Italy? Everyone knows Vesuvius is going to blow again. It's not if; it's when. Ditto with Mount Rainier and the good folk of Seattle-Tacoma. Sure enough, there will be some goofy guy clutching a mike as lava flows his way. I wish I cared.

I had a similar problem with the latest Batman movie, *The Dark*

Knight. I went because I thought my grandson might enjoy it. My tolerance for computer-generated images is getting lower by the minute, so I try to avoid spectacle on the big screen. It's bad enough on CNN hurricane coverage.

There it was—Gotham City in the clutches of the Joker. Everything that could possibly go wrong was going wrong. I watched this noisy hoopla with a mildly detached air and thought, "My stars, the citizens of Gotham City must really be dumb to hang around, movie after movie, for all this turmoil. Are there no U-Hauls in Gotham City? Why don't they just leave?" (Actually, I didn't think, "My stars." It was stronger than that, but this is a family newspaper.)

Of course, once a moviegoer starts mind-wandering like that, it's obvious that she's not being grabbed by noise and fluff created on a green screen. The chances of my ever watching another Batman movie are slim to none.

Here it comes. What this must mean is I am officially entering the "old curmudgeon" era. Or maybe I'm more drawn to reality. Batman, with all its patent silliness, could never unnerve me as much as reading David Halberstam's *The Coldest Winter: America and the Korean War*. The book, so well written, is even more terrifying to me because I knew what happened before I picked it up. I already knew self-absorbed Dougie MacArthur would refuse to believe the Chinese were actually invading Korea. I knew the Eighth Army would be trapped near the border with China and abandoned because of gross ineptitude at the top.

I'm reading the book anyway, partly because my son loaned it to me, and partly because—I'm embarrassed to write this—it's the first Halberstam I've read. He *is* good. Now I'll have to read his Vietnam work, *The Best and the Brightest*.

History isn't knowledge to no purpose. I firmly believe that knowing what people did and why, helps me understand human nature better. I hope it makes me more forgiving of human foible, and more resolved to be a vigilant citizen.

So it goes. Television journalists will continue to dangle from trees and teeter on sea walls, and those citizens of Gotham City will never wise up. Jokers will come and go, but there will never be another book by David Halberstam. Five days after he finished *The Coldest Winter*, Halberstam was killed in a car crash on his way to an interview for his next book. Now that's terrible reality.

DECEMBER 18, 2008

BE MERRY

I'm not a Christmas party person. I'm terrible at small talk and juggling finger food. My idea of a great Christmas is reading favorite Yuletide stories and seeing how much of Luke chapter 2 I can recite from memory. Inhaling fudge, peanut brittle, and toffee is important, too.

I love singing Christmas carols and must publicly admit my envy of the Methodists, who have a hymnal crammed with great carols. My own church's hymnal has a modest amount of favorites, but boy howdy, I wish we had "God Rest Ye Merry Gentlemen" and "We Three Kings" in our book. (I will admit that when I was young, I thought "Orient Are" was a country.)

Christmas feasting may loom large for some of you party animals. I turned to my new book—*Back in the Day: 101 Things Everyone Used to Know How to Do*—for some medieval dining tips.

To begin, you'll know how significant you are by your relationship to the salt bowl, which was placed before the most important guest. Anyone seated below the salt was pretty much second string. This mattered, because everyone washed their hands in a bowl of rose water that was passed down the table. The folks on the end made do with greasy water flecked with questionable debris from the higher-ups.

There were no forks until the later Middle Ages, so dinner guests used spoons, knives, and fingers. The plate, called a trencher, was a slab of stale bread which was gathered up after the meal and given to beggars outside the gates. You might pare off a corner of the bread for yourself but leave the rest for those folks so far below the salt that they are in the street.

Etiquette is not a 20th-century invention. There are certain things you'd better not do at a medieval banquet, or you won't be invited back. Don't blow your nose on the tablecloth, and don't burp in someone's face. (When our kids were growing up, anyone who belched or committed an otherwise unnamed social indiscretion at the table had to shake cream in the gallon jug that I would later work up into butter. Sam still owes me, I think.)

Don't scratch your head, because no one wants your lice on the table. And if your mouth is full, please don't drink out of that communal cup. Keep your thumbs out of the cup, too, and don't pet the dog.

Your companions at table would prefer that you not blow on your soup to cool it, because you might have foul breath. I have to wonder if this is too much of a nicety, considering that few bathed during the Middle Ages. The degree of ripeness was probably so intense that mere halitosis seemed tame.

You are allowed to throw bones and shells on the floor, but make sure you strip most of the meat off those bones. It's also permissible to wipe your fingers on your bread. (If this is the trencher going to beggars, we all know they weren't choosers.) And please don't spit on or over the table.

This reminds me of "The Boar's Head Carol," a favorite Christmas carol sung to this day at Oxford University's Queen's College. It popped up in the 14th century, and we sing the 1521 version today. According to tradition, an Oxford student was walking in a nearby forest, reading Aristotle, when he was attacked by a wild boar. Showing great presence of mind, plus a certain scholarly pragmatism, the student stuffed his copy of Aristotle down the rampaging boar's throat and shouted, "Graecum est," which translated loosely as "It's all Greek to me."

At Queen's and other venues now, the boar's head is carried in on a platter, heralded with music and torchlight. Here's the first verse of the song, which I hum all through the holidays:

"The boar's head in hand bear I,
bedecked with bay and rosemary,
And I pray you my masters be merry,
quo testis in convivio. [As many as are in the feast]
Caput apri defero, reddens laudes Domino."
[The boar's head I offer, giving praises to the Lord.]

Be merry, everyone. No matter how tough times are, we'll prevail by being wise and holding close to family and friends. I've enjoyed writing "Prairie Lite" for the past four years, and will pop in now and then with a few more. Merry Christmas and a Happy New Year from this most wonderful of states.

FAMILY AND EVERYDAY LIFE

DECEMBER 23, 2004

MAKING THAT LIST, CHECKING IT TWICE

I guess I just don't "get" money. There's an inside joke among historians, who have been known to state that they went into history because they didn't understand math. I'm one of those. A few years ago, when I read that Bill Gates's Seattle mansion was going to have more rooms in it than the Sun King's palace at Versailles, my first thought was, "Gee, I'd hate to have to clean that house." One of my kids kindly pointed out to me that if it was *my* house, I would certainly have servants. I hadn't thought of that. I was still trying to wrap my mind around all that vacuuming. Imagine how much Tide-E-Bowl I'd have to install. And I'd probably have to hire Inca runners to backpack the Pledge into distant, interior rooms.

You get the picture. Sad to say, but money puzzles me, mainly because a) I never had any, and b) I'm one of those historians. You'll understand my amusement when I read a recent article in the *Fargo Forum* about the trendy folk with bling and ka-ching who are spending Huge Amounts on Christmas this year. The article warbled on about $1,000 snakeskin handbags, $535 leopard-printed sandals, and $200 jeans adorned with crystals. One retailer was bemoaning the fact that she couldn't keep up with the demand for her mink ponchos, priced upwards of $8,000. Poor thing.

Before my eyes glazed over, I had this grand image of rich kids prostrate and sobbing beside the family tree because the mink ponchos were all gone and they would have to settle for cheap little $2,350 Valentino handbags. I'll have to work on my Christian spirit, because I just didn't feel too sad. In fact, since my husband was in the shower and couldn't hear me, I gave my evil "Mwa-ha-ha" laugh and turned to the comics.

And then between Blondie and Hagar the Horrible, I began to wonder just how happy all this excess could possibly make people who already had too much. This led to asking myself what the greatest gift was that I ever received for Christmas. It took me about five seconds. It was the Christmas two of my grown-up kids gave me books . . . first editions. Two were Kate Seredy's books of children's fiction from a daughter who was in her first years of teaching and earning precious little. The other was Jim Corbett's *The Man-eating Leopard of Rudraprayag* from my son, who was waiting tables to put himself through college.

Through my tears, I realized that they were giving me back a gift I had given them: the gift of reading.

It started with that son, who was a week old and seven pounds when I read him Mark Twain's short story, "The Man Who Corrupted Hadleyburg," during a late-night feeding session. He was just a little guy, so I could nestle him close, hold a book at the same time, and read to him. To this day, he still likes Mark Twain.

When Mary Ruth came along two years later, Jeremy found a spot on the couch or bed where he could listen as I kept reading to him and his new little sister. Through five children altogether, we read through infant feedings, and naptimes, and good times, and sad times, and before bedtimes. (No one ever really objected to bedtime, because it meant another chapter in another book.) We reached a point where, sure, the older ones could read to themselves, but we kept reading anyway. There's nothing better for the soul than to savor Stevenson's *Treasure Island* when it's cold out, and bask in the literary warmth of that distant island on the Spanish Main. And can anything equal descending the Mississippi River with Huck Finn and Jim?

I can still see my kids all crammed around me on the couch, coats close by and lunchboxes at the ready, while someone kept an eye out for the school bus. We read the Great Brain series, and Beverly Cleary's wonderful books about Henry Huggins and his dog, Ribsy, who lived on Klickitat Street in Portland, Oregon. (Imagine our delight a few years later when we discovered, on a trip to Portland to visit friends, that there really *is* a Klickitat Street.) We read it all. We regretted not a minute of that time spent reading, because we were together, and we were having Fun.

Then came Jim Corbett, on the recommendation of my sister who lived in India then. Corbett, born and raised in British India, was a crack shot, game warden, and conservationist who was often hired to stalk and kill man-eating critters that preyed upon villagers. The books were hard to find, but I did locate *The Man-Eater of Kumaon*, which scared us all silly as we sat on the couch waiting for the school bus.

But that was years ago. Imagine my delight when Jeremy found a first edition of the *Man-Eating Leopard of Rudraprayag* and gave it to me for Christmas. It was his thank-you for all those years of reading, and nothing ever made me happier.

Until I opened Mary Ruth's present. She had tracked down Seredy's *The Good Master* and *The Chestry Oak*. (I still wonder how many lunches and things she needed she gave up so I could have those well-loved volumes.) A Hungarian artist, Seredy wrote about her native land just before World War I in *The Good Master*, which she also gorgeously illustrated. I had read that book to my kids, but had never been able to locate *The Chestry Oak*. It's the story of Prince Michael, a young Hungarian royal—orphaned, wounded, and dislocated by World War II—who ends up in a refugee camp and then on a farm in New England. The family thinks his name is Michael Prinz, until it finally dawns on them, through a series of events, just *who* he really is. By now, though, the Russians have taken over his country, and there is no home to return to. All he has left of his past is an acorn from the chestry oak that grew in front of the palace. With his "new" family, he plants the acorn in America. And there is that line, "For yesterday and for all tomorrows, we dance the best we know," that remains with me, because it is so true.

I told my children the story when they were young, and Mary Ruth found it for me, years later. Bliss complete. I have never been better gifted than I was that Christmas. How grateful I am that my mother read to me, and that I read to my own children, and that now they are reading to their children. Like the best gifts, it was free. All it took was the signing of a library card and the wisdom to use it.

Since I already have the best gift, I'll pass on that $8,000 mink poncho from Saks Fifth Avenue and leave it for someone not as fortunate as I am. After all, the holidays are the perfect time to think about those who have less than we do.

JUNE 23, 2005

HOLLYHOCKS, CAMPBELL SOUP, AND MY GRANDMA

When flowers bloom, I think of my Grandma Thacker's bachelor buttons and hollyhocks and her fabulous attic.

Grandma Thacker, my mother's mother, lived in Boise, Idaho. She grew up in Omaha, Nebraska, in posh circumstances as the daughter of a Union Pacific Railroad executive. She received a college education (unlike most women of her era), then married a rascally fellow who eventually ran off, leaving her stranded in Oregon with two young daughters.

I got to know her (two husbands later) when she lived in an old place with a mom-and-pop-type store where the living room would have been. At least it had been a store during the Depression and World War II years. By the time I became aware of her in the early '50s, it was full of junk mainly.

Grandma Thacker never threw anything away. When too much clutter accumulated downstairs, it went into the long attic over a row of apartments she owned next to the store. When we girls visited Grandma, our first stop (after a hug and hello) was the attic. Hollyhocks taller than I was flanked the outside door to the attic. When I see hollyhocks, I think of Grandma.

She saved all of my mother's dolls, even when they were bald, mangled amputees who looked more like the bride of Chucky than pretty playthings. For some strange reason, my mother named all her dolls Rosalee. My sisters and I are grateful she got the name out of her system, so we were not each named Rosalee.

The attic held everything. I'm convinced that if I had dug down deep enough, I'd have found a first draft of the Magna Carta, or maybe a note from Noah to his sons, reminding them to pick up a manure fork for the ark.

What I did find, when I was old enough to care, were yellowing love letters to my mom from a fellow named Gordon Barrett. He was a high school classmate who went to California for college while she stayed behind in Boise to go to junior college.

To my disappointment, they were pretty ordinary letters. To make it worse, all Mom remembered (or cared to tell me about Gordon) was that he had bad breath. What those letters did tell me was that my mother actually had a life before she became my mother. To a child, that's a revelation.

Probably the coolest thing about Grandma Thacker's old rattletrap house was her bathroom, with its built-in bookcase surrounding the toilet. It's my contention that no one using that toilet and taking advantage of the library to read and (um) relax would ever develop hemorrhoids.

After one of our visits to Grandma Thacker, she and I started corresponding. I still appreciate her patience in writing to a little girl who probably didn't have much to say, and who was learning the rudiments of sentences. We wrote faithfully to each other for years.

One thing that tickled me about her letters, even as it embarrassed my mother, was that Grandma wrote to me on anything she had at hand. Never wasteful, she wrote on the backs of Campbell Soup labels: long, thin letters in her loopy handwriting. No one else I knew got Campbell Soup letters. Mmm, mmm good.

Grandma T was a ragtag, Bohemian lady with scraggly hair and stockings that were always falling down. She hadn't a clue how to marry well, and never lived the genteel life she had been born into. I never heard a complaint, though, so I think it was what she wanted.

I like to think—or at least hope—that I inherited her lively mind. I did end up with a small gold flower pin with a seed pearl centered in the petal, and a gold watch such as ladies back then pinned to their shirtwaists. The watch came with its case and a note from her father: "To my darling, sweet sixteen." What a nice dad. What a sweet note.

I suppose she planted bachelor buttons because she liked them. I used to plant them, too, to remind me of her. I haven't done that in a while, but I'm wondering now, is it too late this season to plant bachelor buttons?

Tonight I'll write my grandson a letter on the back of a Campbell Soup label. I do know this: his mother won't be embarrassed.

JUNE 30, 2005

ROOMS AND APES IN CODY, WYOMING

My Baier grandparents (my dad's folks) lived in Cody, Wyoming. They were polar opposites of my Grandma Thacker, with her casual ways.

One of the earliest certified mechanics of the automotive era, Grandpa stumbled upon Cody when he and his brother-in-law traveled west from Minnesota in 1926 or '27 in search of a healthier climate for Grandpa, who had asthma.

The high, dry air of Cody suited him fine, and he was instantly employable as a mechanic. He sent for Grandma and the kids, and they settled down in what was still essentially a frontier town. Buffalo Bill Cody had founded the town in 1905 and named it after himself.

My Aunt Marie, Grandpa's oldest child, remembers living in a tent for three weeks until they were able to find a house to rent. Grandpa later bought a boarding house. He called it "Baier Rooms and Apts.," but my Montana cousins named it "Baier Rooms and Apes." Some of the boarders were cowboys who worked on local ranches until winter came. Other men worked on construction crews. One old gent named Boxcar Murphy used to share his swiss cheese with me and tell stories.

During the Korean War when Dad was stationed in Thailand, Mom, Karen, and I moved to Cody to live in Baier Rooms and Apes. Grandpa had built several cottages behind the boarding house, and we rented one of those. I wasn't in school yet, but I recall a few things.

During late fall, my Montana cousins came to visit. David (I think he was 5) convinced Karen and me to join him in a junkyard heist, where we acquired a handful of windshield wipers. David thought we should sell those wipers, so we dragged a box to Sheridan Avenue and set up shop.

I do remember Karen was wearing an old sweater held together with a safety pin. It was cold and windy, and we must have looked pretty pathetic. Whenever I think of Hans Christian Andersen's story "The Little Match Girl," my mind goes to Karen in that ragged sweater, peddling windshield wipers.

I remember someone paid David 20 cents for a wiper, not bad money in 1951. Someone else must have alerted my grandparents to the urchins selling contraband, because we were whisked away and encouraged not to do that again.

That must have embarrassed my grandparents, who were exemplary townsfolk. Grandpa was chief of the volunteer fire department, and Grandma was a great joiner. At one time or other, she belonged to every women's club in Cody. She was even president of the Past Presidents' Club once, which tickled me to no end.

One of my earliest memories of Grandma was her fur piece. It was a fox stole with black glass eyes and paws dangling down. I was 4 then, and on eye level with those beady orbs. I remember standing in a crowd one night with Grandma, my face mashed against those beady eyes. It didn't cause any nightmares that I remember, but I still have a healthy respect for animals, dead or alive, draped around people's necks.

Grandma was stylish. We called her the Jewelry Grandma because she had enormous quantities of costume jewelry, especially clip-on earrings. She didn't mind if we tried them on, but my stars, I wonder how she could stand so much pain on her earlobes. From an early age, I have associated fashion with pain. (Make something of that, Freud!)

I have another memory of Baier Rooms and Apes, that winter when Dad was so far away in Bangkok, Thailand. He sent us an 8 mm home movie in his Christmas box. Grandpa set up the projector, and in the flickering light, we saw exotic sights far beyond our frontier town in Wyoming: Buddhist monks in saffron robes, life-sized demon warrior statues, houseboats on the canals, men wrestling a python in a basket.

Dad was in the film at the end, riding in a rickshaw and waving to his little girls so far away. We waved back to the wall, excited to know that even in snowy Wyoming, so close to Yellowstone Park, our dad was only a grainy flicker away on the wall of Baier Rooms and Apes.

JULY 14, 2005

I'LL TAKE CARE OF HIM, MOM, I PROMISE

My daughter Liz bought a hamster recently. She got a plastic hamster ball to put him in. Now he gets a workout rolling around in her apartment. The hamster is faring much better than Liz's goldfish, which usually just move in to go belly up. I mean, when fish see Liz looming over them in the pet store, they probably let out primal screams we can't hear. It's harsh.

Maybe the hamster reminds Liz of her childhood, when we had hamsters. I recall at least one litter of hamster babies, which we sold to the pet store. I never mentioned to my kids that baby hamsters often end up purchased as pet food for snakes. That admission would have branded me as a Bad Mother.

Any mother will identify: The kids promised to tend the hamsters, but soon enough, the hamsters became my responsibility. I suppose I should have complained, but I really didn't mind the little guys.

I take that back; I did mind them when they escaped. This happened several times, and for some weird reason, the hamsters always came looking for me.

Maybe it was because I was their caregiver, which probably made me God in their little eyes and even littler brains. They always seemed to find me at night, when I was asleep. They'd tiptoe across my pillow and whisper, "Feed me, oh Great One," in my ear.

The first time it happened I nearly stopped breathing. Maybe I don't sleep well even now, because I'm still on alert for hamsters on my pillow. Some women get chocolates on their pillows; I get hamsters.

My dad fared better with his pets. Like many folks in Cody, the Baiers raised chickens. Dad ended up with a rooster he named Rudolph, which he taught to ride on the handlebars of his bike. "I tied a little rope around his leg to retrieve him in case he fell off," Dad told me. "He hardly ever did."

Rudolph came to a sad end. When the Baiers got rid of their poultry, Rudolph went out in a blaze of glory as chicken and dumplings. "It bothered me," Dad admitted.

At various times in his youth, Dad had three dogs: Teaser I, Tippy, and Teaser II. One of the Teasers had a long, wavy tail. Teaser was the only dog in town to figure out how to use his tail to open the electric eye door at the Cody Trading Company.

That may have been the same Teaser who achieved lasting fame for loyalty above and beyond the call of duty. It was almost a Jack London story. One winter day, Dad rode his bike to school. As usual, Teaser settled down by the bike to guard it and wait for school to end.

A blizzard struck, and school let out early. Grandpa picked up Dad, so they bypassed the bike rack. Teaser curled up tighter and spent the night guarding the bike. For his efforts, Teaser the Wonder Dog got his photo in the Cody Enterprise.

We had cats when I was growing up. They've blended together in my mind through the years, but I learned young to put my money on a cat in a fight. One of my earliest California memories is of our cat—claws dug in deep—riding on the back of a terrified dog that thought to pass through our yard. Silly dog.

Another of my parents' cats liked to hide marbles, then haul them out after everyone was in bed. The cat would bat those marbles down the hall. In the middle of the night, it sounded like bowling balls.

Cookie, a Kelly cat, was a personal favorite. She was a bit aloof and took to striking out on her own whenever the mood grabbed her. We called those impromptu junkets Cookie's "business trips." She'd come back after a few days, but never did bore us with vacation photos.

In 1990, we moved to Louisiana from Missouri, and Cookie came, too. We kept her indoors long enough for her to get used to the idea, then let her out.

And that was the last time we saw Cookie. Personally, I think she wanted to go home to Missouri, and probably did. Can't blame her. Considering how bad Louisiana turned out, we should have gone, too. Maybe animals just know.

JULY 21, 2005

IF YOU HAD AN AUNT LIKE MINE

I just got home from a weekend in Worden, Montana, visiting my Trask cousins, children of Marie and Preston Trask. As fun as it was to see them, I know we were all missing Marie, their mom and my aunt.

She was ordinary like us—a retired nurse, mother of eight, wife of a former rancher—but with one extraordinary skill. I don't know how she did it, but each of us (kids and cousins) was convinced that we were her favorite.

Maybe it was the way she so totally focused on us when we were in her orbit. When Aunt Marie talked to me, or shared a recipe of hers, or made me a dress or blouse, I knew she cared totally and only for me.

Why does a child hunger to know that he or she is the special one? When we're old enough to think rationally about the matter, or maybe when we have children of our own, we realize there is plenty of love to go around. Still, maybe some part of us wants to be the only one, the loved one.

I asked my cousin Margaret about this knack of her mother's to make each son, daughter, and niece feel completely special. "Oh, yes," Margaret told me with a straight face. "I was her favorite child."

We all were. What a gift.

Aunt Marie also gave me the best recipe for peanut brittle. Let me inject a modest aside here: I make the best peanut brittle in the world, thanks to Aunt Marie's recipe. I have the secret for making it an unparalleled culinary event. I'll be happy to demonstrate someday when atmospheric conditions are just right, and Jupiter is aligned with Mars.

Come to think of it, I use her fudge recipe, too. I have children who would probably commit barbaric acts just for Aunt Marie's fudge.

Aunt Marie and William Clark will always be bound together in my mind and heart. I was reminded of that last Friday when we drove by Pompey's Pillar, some 25 miles east of Billings.

As Lewis & Clark fans know, Pompey's Pillar is where Clark left the only physical reminder of the journey, carving his name and the date there when he came down the Yellowstone River in 1806. He called the butte Pompey's Tower after his nickname of Pomp for Sakakawea's son Jean Baptiste Charbonneau, who accompanied the expedition as a baby. Nicholas Biddle, who first edited the journals, changed it to Pompey's Pillar.

Aunt Marie loved the history of her Rocky Mountain region. Whenever we Baier cousins visited the ranch, she always made a point to take us picnicking or to a state park. The most mundane activities became events, mainly because Aunt Marie wanted her favorite niece (me) to have a good time.

I went to see her in Worden a year or so before she died. She was nearly bent double with osteoporosis and had serious difficulty getting around, but she was as sharp and wonderful as ever.

Before I left, she took my hand in hers, looked into my eyes, and told me in her raspy voice, "Next time you come back, we'll pack a picnic lunch and visit Pompey's Pillar." Since I was her favorite niece, I knew she meant it; I assured her we would do that.

In December 1999, I received word from my dad that Aunt Marie died in her sleep. My sisters (who each thought she was the favorite niece) flew to Billings from Minneapolis and Orlando. I drove over, thinking of Aunt Marie all the way.

As I came to the Pompey's Pillar exit, I took the off ramp on impulse and stopped in the parking lot. It wasn't snowing, but it was cold. The Bureau of Land Management administers the national landmark, but everything was shut down for the winter.

No matter; I didn't want to walk up the boardwalk trail and look at William Clark's signature. Aunt Marie had promised me that we would see it together on my next visit. She wasn't there anymore, so I couldn't go. Favorite nieces are polite and wait.

OCTOBER 6, 2005

NO BEARS, NO BEARS AT ALL

Jeremy the Border Patrol guy called last week from Montana with a real story. He claims it's true. He heard it from a game warden on the Blackfeet Reservation, who says he saw the whole thing happen at Glacier National Park. Who am I to doubt?

It seems a tourist from back East went into a store in the park and bought a can of bear repellent. He took the can and his family into the parking lot, lined them up, and sprayed them.

Apparently he thought bear spray worked like insect repellent. Oops, no. His whole family went to the hospital. I only hope, when she recovered, that his wife got a good lawyer and lots of lovely alimony.

Jeremy's been on the Montana-Canadian border for a year now. This summer, he decided to walk his area along that imaginary line. He hiked a little each day, and now he's done. He had bear sightings, but none were too close.

The Border Patrol wouldn't issue bear spray, and he's too cheap to buy it, so he checked out a shotgun each day and took that along. He called it bear spray.

Because inquiring minds want to know, I had to look up bear spray on the Internet. I learned there are several varieties, and all claim to repel bears by spraying it at the bear and not, um, on oneself.

One spray claimed it was "university-tested" at the University of Montana. Yikes. Maybe the best way to avoid bears is to stay away from the University of Montana, since they seem to be on campus. That's almost a no-brainer.

Another spray, called "Guard Alaska," is manufactured in Maryland and New Jersey. New Jersey? Would you trust bear spray from a state with more Mafiosi than wildlife? The other brands were manufactured in Arizona and Missouri. I'm skeptical.

Jeremy hasn't seen a bear up really close yet, and he'd like to keep it that way. We do have a common bear experience, though, through a book. It started when I was a little girl, and my mother read me Alice Dalgliesh's story "The Bears on Hemlock Mountain."

It's about Jonathan, 8 years old, who is sent over Hemlock Mountain to borrow a big iron pot from his aunt. He's heard rumors about bears, but his mother tells him, "There are no bears, no bears at all, on Hemlock Mountain."

Jonathan hurries over the mountain. What with one thing and another, he doesn't start back until dusk, lugging that iron pot. He keeps repeating, "No bears, no bears at all," over and over until (gulp) he sees a bear. Not one, but two.

Because he is a resourceful pioneer boy, Jonathan tips the iron pot on top of himself and hides underneath. It's a great book for children, because it's a little bit scary, but everything turns out all right.

My mom read it to me; I read it to my children, starting with Jeremy. When my first grandchild was old enough, I bought a copy, taped myself reading it, and mailed book and tape to him in San Diego. Maybe someday he'll read it to his children.

That's as close as I want to get to a bear. No force on earth will drag me to that new documentary, *Grizzly Man*. It's the sad saga of bear activist Timothy Treadwell, who cavorted (briefly) among Alaskan grizzlies. He and his friend Amie Huguenard were romping with the bears as usual when, uh-oh, everything went south in a bad way.

Treadwell had videotape and audiotape running during the whole thing. Luckily, nothing appears on the videotape. The audiotape recorded the attack from beginning to lunch.

Treadwell was probably a nut to begin with, even though he managed to survive among the bears for several years. Funny thing about bears: When it goes bad with bears, there's no middle ground.

So if you're out in bear country this fall, remember to make lots of noise as you walk those trails. If you happen to surprise a bear, back away slowly and don't make eye contact. Assume a non-threatening posture. If a bear attacks and you have bear spray, use it on the bear.

And if you happen to be in Missoula, for heaven's sake, stay away from the University of Montana.

DECEMBER 22, 2005

THE ONE AND ONLY FAMOUS AIR TREE

I'm not a big fan of poverty, but if we hadn't been broke one Christmas, the Famous Air Tree never would have happened.

I put up the Famous Air Tree in Louisiana, Missouri, and a couple of times here in North Dakota, but no more. I'm not a big fan of climbing ladders, either, and the air tree depends on ceilings.

This story starts in Monroe, Louisiana, and one Christmas my husband was highly underemployed. (Can't think of anything nice to write about Louisiana, except that the food is so good. Don't push me on this one, folks. I'm apt to snarl.)

I had a part-time job, and times wuz tuff. We still had two children living at home. I asked them if they wanted me to buy a Christmas tree that year, or spend the tree money on more presents.

They wanted presents, of course, but they also wanted a Christmas tree. I'm not particularly creative, but desperation sometimes breeds creativity.

Maybe I was thinking about "The Emperor's New Clothes," or maybe about the Whos down in Whoville, but as I stared at the place where the tree would go—if we could have afforded one—I had an epiphany.

What if we pretended a Christmas tree? I could hang ornaments from the ceiling, about where I'd hang them if I were decorating a tree.

I bought some fishing line and clear pushpins. I tied a test ornament to a length of the line, and secured the line to the ceiling with a tack. The colorless line against the white wall made the ornament appear to be hanging in midair, connected to nothing. It was an amazing special effect. The air tree was born.

I spent the afternoon on the ladder, arranging the ornaments at varying levels, as I would have if there had been an actual tree there to support them. At the top near the ceiling went the cornhusk angel from Miss D, my Texas journalism teacher, given to me the Christmas before her sudden death.

I've never seen a more stunning non-tree, something created out of bitterness and sorrow at the illegal way my husband had been treated by his former employer. I didn't realize it right then, but that tree was the healthiest thing that had happened in a while. It made me smile.

My sense of humor was back. I put the metal tree holder underneath the air tree and filled it with water. The cats loved that. Come to think of it, they loved batting around the ornaments without a tree in the way.

We discovered other benefits to the Famous Air Tree. There weren't any pine needles to vacuum. No one was allergic to it. Everyone, including neighbors, enjoyed it.

Surmising the air tree needed lightweight ornaments, Denise Grayson from down the block gifted us with miniature wooden soldiers. She's also the one who named the Famous Air Tree, I do believe.

Chuck Pryor from next door came over to see if he could string some lights in the air. He resolved to try something with fiber optics next year. (A few years later, our oldest daughter did manage to hang some lights from her air tree.)

I built the air tree for several Christmases in Louisiana, then we moved to Missouri, where life improved. When I suggested to my girls one December that we could afford a real tree again, you'd have thought I was asking them to walk barefoot through broken glass.

"Mom! We have to have the air tree!"

So we did, through several more Christmases. It ended last year. I was tired of climbing that ladder and leaning out to make sure the fishing line didn't tangle. Menard's was selling a little artificial tree for $9.95. That's what I wanted.

It was so easy to decorate. I retired Miss D's cornhusk angel because she was wearing out. The two wooden states of Texas went up again, along with the chili peppers, and the little wreaths and snowmen I had spent a whole year crocheting.

It's a beautiful tree, too. I miss the Famous Air Tree, but I won't forget what it taught me about grit, resourcefulness, and hanging on five minutes longer than the crisis.

June 29, 2006

SHOULD AULD ACQUAINTANCE BE FORGOT?

I'm descended from a long line of Fergussons. How long, I had no idea until I visited Chatfield, Minnesota, recently.

I have two sisters: Wanda in St. Paul and Karen in Orlando. We're busy—they're world travelers—and it's hard to get together. We decided to meet in St. Paul and drive to Chatfield, 20 miles southeast of Rochester.

We had other plans, too, but we spent more of our visit in Chatfield, admiring a huge barn built in 1881 by our great-great-grandfather Thomas Fergusson, a stonemason from Kirkcudbright, Scotland. We saw houses, a town hall, and a school he built, too.

Thomas was born in 1841 and sailed to the United States in 1869 with his brother-in-law William McVinnie. His wife, Jean, and two children—one of them my Great-Grandpa Sam—followed a year later.

Family lore says they came with others from Kirkcudbright and brought their Presbyterian minister along. My Aunt Marie remembered them as relatives with thick accents. We joked about that, saying no Chatfield neighbor could understand more than one word in 10. It was likely so; some Scots accents are impenetrable.

I never thought I would ever fall in love with a barn, but what a barn: 100 feet long, 40 feet wide, and three stories tall. Thomas built it of limestone right next to the road that led to his stone house behind. Twenty years later, he built the other half of the barn on the other side of the road, and joined the two with a stone center section arching over the road. Records say that although family members helped Thomas haul the stones up to each higher level, he placed each one himself.

The Fergusson farm passed to other hands many years ago. To our good fortune, it's now owned by Gary and Debby Anderson, who love it.

They have collected photos and documents relating to the Fergussons and love to talk about their home.

When they acquired it, the house had been empty for years. They could have torn it down, but they restored it. They recently reroofed the barn, which must have been a monumental undertaking, considering the height. I get queasy just thinking about it.

There's farm equipment in the barn, but the main inhabitants are swallows. *Inside* the barn is the silo, a round stone structure looking like a castle tower. I wish I could convey the massive size of that building. Barricaded and supplied, we probably could have held off the whole German Sixth Army at Stalingrad.

Following Debby's directions, we stopped at the other stone buildings Thomas built that are still in use. I hope Thomas knows that his 1877 township hall—square and elegant without a stone out of line—is where everyone still votes.

We drove to the Scottish cemetery. The stone church Thomas built was destroyed in a tornado in 1903, but there are headstones marking Fergusson, McVinnie, and McGhie relatives, and some Baiers, too, from the German side of the family.

These are my people. I know what they look like, too. The Andersons had remarked several times how much we resembled their old photographs of the Fergussons. In fact, Gary broke off conversation more than once to exclaim, "I can't get over how much you look like them."

Words fail me. I can't explain what this all means to three sisters who were raised here and there, courtesy of the US Navy. We never had any roots until we went to Chatfield.

Fergusson genes are strong. Karen's son, Alok, has black hair like his father, Narsingh, but he looks just like my dad. The Andersons would really do a double take if they could see Alok Krishna Deo, born in Kanpur, India, who's a dead ringer for Thomas Fergusson from Scotland.

Funny how life is. I never knew I could love people I have never met, until I stood in that enormous barn in rural Chatfield, a monument to a real artist. And if that wasn't enough, my sisters informed me in the barn that next year for my birthday, the three of us are going to Kirkcudbright, Scotland.

We're going to that fishing village on Solway Firth, part of the ancient kingdom of Galloway (ruled, incidentally, by a Fergusson). I think we'll find more elegant, square buildings without a stone off plumb, like Thomas himself. Like us, too, if we're lucky.

AUGUST 31, 2006

RUB A DUB DUB

When I was in the post office recently, I picked up a pamphlet. I generally pick up free stuff with writing on it. You never know when you might be stuck in a long line, or maybe road construction, and need something to read, especially if there's not a flagger to talk to.

The pamphlet was titled "USPS Anti-Money Laundering Program." It wasn't deathless prose, but it got me thinking about money and other things I have laundered.

I've sent a lot of stuff through the laundry, especially when my kids were younger. I know a good *hausfrau* is supposed to check all pockets before washing clothes, but I'm a coward. If the glop in the sink trap makes me squeamish, why would I stick my hand in a kid's pocket?

I remember a small frog once, much the worse for wear after the spin cycle. I did the thumb and forefinger fireman's carry and deposited him on a bed of dryer lint, where he—ahem—croaked.

Sometimes there was money in those pockets, but not often. None of us ever had much, so we were fairly careful with it. Now and then, there'd be a dollar or two when the kids were in high school. Because I know my kids worked pretty hard for their money, I generally tried to locate the owner.

Not so with coins. I figured they were my tip for doing all that laundry. Especially quarters. It is said that everyone has a price. I'm embarrassed to admit that my price goes no higher than quarters. (Of course, I'm the woman who, when asked what she wanted if she could have anything, said "A ham on Easter." Sheesh, what an idiot. This makes me a really cheap date.)

Part of this may be due to my motto: "Expect nothing." Now don't roll your eyes. It's really a serviceable motto that wards off a lot of disappointment, and makes the good stuff even cooler when it actually happens. And it always does; maybe I'm a pessimistic optimist.

Let me illustrate. In 1958 when we lived on one of Georgia's beautiful Sea Islands, I entered a poetry contest and won second prize.

The award was $10, a tidy sum in 1958. I remember one thing I bought with the money: a light blue raincoat. It had metal clasps and deep pockets.

Great raincoat. I wore it through the island's rainy season, and then put it away for the summer. Summers are long in South Georgia. It was many months later when I got the raincoat out of the closet again.

I wore it to school and at some point, put my hand in the pocket. I pulled out a dollar bill and 15 cents. That was 48 years ago, and I still remember the exact amount and how pleased I was.

Maybe I like the thrill of finding something unexpected: not of the spin-cycle frog carcass variety, but something really keen. I enjoyed Easter egg hunts long after the thrill of that should have worn off.

My favorite unexpected treasure was Hale-Bopp Comet, which revisited our corner of the universe for an amazing 18 months in 1996–1997. The last time it was visible on earth was during the time of the pharaohs in ancient Egypt.

That fact was enough to send me into the yard every night during that winter and early spring of 1997. I was staring at history, at something last seen by Egyptians who walked funny on tomb paintings.

It was an unexpected pleasure beyond anything I can remember. I've always enjoyed the night sky, and I can identify some of the constellations. When Hale-Bopp arrived with its brightness and long twin tails, it was totally alien in that sky I thought I knew so well. I suppose I had taken the night sky for granted. Here was this gorgeous visitor from another corner of my universe. Where had it been all my life?

I watched it every night. I welcomed it, I enjoyed it, and I was sorry when it finally headed back to other distant ports of call.

It'll be back in 4380. I hope someone is here to see Hale-Bopp again. I'm not sure why that raises a lump in my throat, except that I wish it could be me. Not bad for the woman who expects nothing. I just want the universe.

OCTOBER 19, 2006

"THE STAG AT EVE HAD DRUNK HIS FILL"

It amazes me that one of life's thorniest tasks is assigned to amateurs. I refer to child rearing.

I think my daughter Mary Ruth has a leg up on the whole process. She is a special education teacher, so there isn't much her three munchkins can do that she hasn't already seen.

I remember one time she had me and her dad going nuts, which only demonstrates what absolute ninnies that poor child had to live with during her growing up years.

She was two and we were in Wyoming, and I remember that bathroom vividly. She pointed to the three-level shelf over the toilet and demanded, "Keem!"

We took item after item off the shelves as her frustration only escalated. We sure weren't producing "Keem!" She was red-faced and headed for the Cowboy State's greatest meltdown.

We practically dismantled the bathroom, and still she kept crying and pointing. Finally, oh, finally, I grabbed the hand lotion. That was it. All she wanted was a little hand keem. Sheesh, what idiot parents.

There are wiser parents. When we lived in Louisiana, our friend Jeff Johnson took us to dinner at his parents' house. I don't remember how it came up, but Jeff's dad told us how his father used to deal with sibling squabbling when he and his sister started picking on each other.

He'd hand his son and daughter a burlap bag and point to the cotton field. They each had to pick a sack full of cotton before they could come back in the house. Jeff's dad laughed about it when he told us the story, but he remembered that his anger was always long over before those sacks were full. If that's not a deterrent to a childish argument, I can't imagine what is, considering the length and depth of humid, hot Louisiana summers.

Sometimes parents do unwitting stuff that means nothing to them, but their children never forget it.

My mom was careful about our appearance. She didn't like smudges on her daughters' faces. It only became an issue when we were out of the house and on our way somewhere in public.

If she noticed some facial boo-boo, she'd pull a limp tissue from the depths of her handbag, moisten it with her saliva, and scrub away. Maybe all moms do that. Trouble was, she liked to chew Dentyne gum. To this day, that cinnamon aroma makes me cringe.

When I had kids, I vowed a mighty vow that I wouldn't do the spit bath thing. I generally didn't, which means sometimes my darlings looked more like orcs than tidy, textbook children. At least I saved them from a lifelong aversion to cinnamon-flavored gum.

We got one thing right, though. When our kids were small, we discovered the brilliance of using washcloths instead of paper napkins at mealtime. (I still do it, but not with company and the good china. Honest.)

Parents, you know how it is. Invariably, some kid will tip over milk or juice. Instead of hollering at the poor spiller for being a kid, we all just tossed our washcloth napkins in the direction of the spill. The mess was absorbed quickly, and no one got a pointless lecture.

Parenting—or grandparenting—can be poetry. When I was young, my mother, sisters, and I stopped in Rochester, Minnesota, to visit my father's grandfather, Sam Fergusson, in a nursing home.

When we came into his room, I noticed a painting of a stag over his bed. Grandma Belle told him Mickey's wife and kids were there to say hello.

He must have thought my dad was there, too, because he started to recite a verse from Sir Walter Scott's poem, "The Lady of the Lake:"

"The stag at eve had drunk his fill,
When danced the moon on Monan's rill,
And deep his midnight lair had made,
In lone Glenartney's hazel shade."

It's a long poem from Scotland's highlands. Grandpa Sam, who was born in Scotland, used to sit my dad on his lap and recite "The Stag at Eve" to him.

And there Grandpa Sam was, old now, reciting that poem in his hospital bed, wishing to see the absent Mickey. Tears ran down his cheeks and he couldn't finish. Grandpa Sam died a few years later. I have that painting now.

Grandpa Sam Fergusson got it entirely right: a beloved grandson, a lap, poetry.

OCTOBER 26, 2006

DR. YUNUS, YOU'RE MY HERO

Reading the newspaper or a news magazine is so discouraging lately that I try to peek through my fingers with my hands over my eyes while I read.

News is scary: insurgents insurging as only they can. And when it's not scary, it's stupid: rich airhead celebrities who labor under the delusion that we care about their opinions.

Imagine my pleasure recently to read that Muhammad Yunus won the Nobel Peace Prize.

He's my hero, and has been for years. I've wondered how long it would be before Yunus won a Nobel Prize for peace or economics. How about both? Every year?

The prize was $1.4 million, divided between Yunus and his Grameen Bank. He's using his share to finance research to create high-protein, low-cost food for the poor. The Grameen Bank portion of his win will create an eye clinic in Bangladesh.

Yunus is from Bangladesh, maybe the poorest place on earth. For years, poor folk just trying to put one meal a day on the table for their kids were ground under by predatory money lenders, if they wanted a small loan to start a business.

We're not talking million dollar loans to start General Motors. How about $15 to buy enough string to make a few shopping bags?

In 1974, Dr. Yunus, an economist, started the Grameen Bank ("Bank of the Villages"), when he reached in his own pocket and loaned $27 to 43 families, so they could make small items to sell. They had no collateral, and he didn't ask for any. All he asked was for them to pay it back when they could.

That was precisely what happened. The loan was repaid 100 percent. Heartened by the experiment, which only proved what he already believed about the sincerity of the rural poor, Yunus began the Grameen Bank.

He extended what is now called "microcredit" mainly to women. He understood mothers and their commitment to feeding, clothing, and educating their children. He knew moms wouldn't be casual about loans. Too much is at stake, especially in dirt-poor Bangladesh, where catastrophe is never more than a typhoon away.

His faith in women never wavered. Grameen Bank loans have an unheard-of 98 percent payback rate. Since 1974, Grameen Banks have spread across Bangladesh, numbering 2,100 now.

Things slowed down a little in 1995, when some religious fundamentalist pinheads objected to a bank dedicated to improving the status of women. Their boycott fizzled. (Nice try, guys.)

Microcredit has spread around the world, including the United States. It may vary a little in form, but the core remains constant. If you make a small loan to a resourceful woman with a plan, she will work hard—so hard—to create something to sell.

She will pay back that loan, and maybe get another $20 loan to expand her business. She'll pay that back, too, because the stakes are astronomically high—the survival of her children.

This is little stuff: school lunch money stuff. One clever woman in Bangladesh took out a Grameen loan for a cell phone. The country has few phones. For pennies, she lets people in her village make telephone calls. How simple is that? How brilliant?

A woman in the Philippines makes colorful and sturdy bags with used paper drink containers. All she needed was a loan to buy a treadle sewing machine. Now many of her village friends work for her, making those brave little bags. We own one. (She's my hero, too.)

Dr. Yunus has become a fashionista, of sorts. No Armani suits, though. He wears what is known now as Grameen check, a loose cotton fabric woven on Bangladeshi looms in rural villages.

The weavers got their business boost through Grameen Bank. They're thriving, and earning money doing what they're good at. People all over the world buy this fabric now.

Next semester, the "What in the World" group at Valley City State University will be showing "Small Fortunes," a remarkable film exploring microcredit in many nations. I wish the group could make attendance mandatory for everyone in Valley City.

There's one problem with the film. It's the same problem Dr. Yunus comes across everywhere: Your heart might be touched and you might experience an overwhelming urge to donate a few dollars to the Grameen Bank.

Don't resist. It's chump change for us, and life or death for poor, hardworking women.

DECEMBER 21, 2006
THE GIFT HORSE HAS A BIG MOUTH

I know we're supposed to believe it's always better to give than to receive, but I love getting gifts.

It started early. My favorite childhood Christmas gift was a toy farm. Santa brought it that Christmas we spent in Cody, Wyoming, while my dad was overseas in Thailand and I was four.

The best part of it was Mr. Kaiser, even though I don't think the little metal cowboy figure came with the farm. Even city slicker tunesmiths like Rogers and Hammerstein knew cowboys and farmers didn't get along: "Don't treat him like a louse, make him welcome in your house, but be sure that you lock up your wife and daughters."

Anyway, someone gave me a cowboy figure about three inches tall, complete with batwing chaps and a ten-gallon hat. He just naturally gravitated to the toy farm. He was Mr. Kaiser because that was the name of my grandparents' friend, who was—or had been—a genuine cowboy.

He belonged to the Boot and Bottle Club in Cody, and rode a black horse. I remember mornings when Mr. Kaiser loped over on his horse to Grandma's kitchen window, where he'd lean down and hand her a pint of cream.

I kept that figurine for years, but don't know what happened to it. I remember Mr. Kaiser, though, and always think of him around the holidays, when I remember gifts of Christmas Past.

Other than Mr. Kaiser, my favorite gifts will always be books, as I have mentioned before. The books my kids have given me—favorite, hard-to-find ones we read earlier, mom to kid—are more than books, because they say something significant about the gift of literacy.

My son Jeremy and I have settled into a pleasant Christmas routine. We buy each other a book, and they have to be books we would both enjoy, because as soon as we're done, we exchange them.

He was easy this year. We both read an excerpt from a new history of the Battle of Leyte Gulf and knew we wanted the whole book. I just happened to be quicker on the Amazon trigger finger than he was.

My kids are nothing if not clever. Back when Mary Ruth was attending Brigham Young University, paying her own way, and going hungry sometimes, she knew what to do with those ridiculously expensive textbooks she had to purchase.

If you buy something at the BYU Bookstore, you can have it gift wrapped for free. After Mary Ruth plunked down her hard-earned cash for each semester's overpriced texts, she took them to the gift-wrapping counter and had each one wrapped for free.

I admire people like Mary Ruth who make the best of unfortunate situations. In all the books I've read, nowhere is that kind of defiant courage more evident than in Laura Ingalls Wilder's little book *The First Four Years*.

This is the story of what happened after *These Happy Golden Years*, when she and Almanzo were married. It's a tough time, with illness, crop failure, fire, and death.

The wheat crop was doing well, until a hailstorm stretched it flatter than a boot camp bunk. Without a word, Almanzo went outside, gathered the hailstones, and made ice cream.

On the Richter scale of courage, the above paragraph requires no additional commentary.

For Christmas one year, Mary Ruth gave me a book called *Pioneer Women: The Lives of Women on the Frontier*. In it, Oregon pioneer Martha Gay Masterson told this story of her small son Freddie. She had cut his hair for the first time and asked him what she should do with the clippings.

Freddie told her to keep a lock for herself and put the rest outside for the birds. She did; he died suddenly a few days later.

That fall, her daughter called her outside to look at an abandoned nest. There, among the twigs and leaves, were Freddie's golden curls.

Martha Gay kept that nest among her treasured possessions, a little gift from a son who died too young, an all-too-common condition on the frontier.

When my daughter Liz was young, she gave me a metal clown keychain for Christmas. I still use it, and think of her every time I start my car.

That's not all. I think of our five children many times a day, because they're the best gift we have.

FEBRUARY 1, 2007

CALLING ALL MOTHERS

When my five children were young, I wasn't sure there was a time when they would prove useful to me. I loved them, but they were lots of work, and I'm naturally lazy.

(You can already tell from this beginning that I am not going to get a Mother of the Year award in this lifetime.)

I wrote my first novel in 1984, mostly by getting up early and writing in the laundry room before anyone woke up and wanted something.

When my kids were older, I would occasionally write at the kitchen table. This was not wholly successful, but at least I knew where they were.

It's not easy to write with kids running around. I was tempted to dedicate *Marian's Christmas Wish* this way: *To my children—I wrote this in spite of you.*

I didn't. I want them to put me in a good nursing home some day.

But they've grown up and so have I. Jeremy gave me a column idea, so I've found another good use for my offspring.

He wrote: "Our conversation earlier gave me an idea for a column. You could do one on all the weird things people have telephoned to ask you."

By people, he mostly means himself and his sibs. He's right; there have been some doozies.

When Jeremy and his sister Mary Ruth were in college, they would both call with this plea: "Mom, tell me to study."

This was usually delivered in a fake whine, perhaps so I would appreciate that they were no longer three years old.

We enjoyed the tell-me-to-study calls. I assume they studied after we hung up, because they both graduated.

Now I get calls of this nature: "Mom, tell me to clean the house."

I can count on recipe calls around the holidays, usually involving an artery-clogger they call "cheesy potatoes."

We call it "funeral potatoes" in the South. I don't know what you call it here, but it involves shredded potatoes, sour cream, cream of mushroom soup, chopped green onions, butter, and lots of cheese. All the basic food groups.

No one ever remembers the recipe, or maybe they wrote it with disappearing ink, so someone invariably phones home. I grumble, make Mom noises, and tell them to write it down this time, but they never do.

Thank goodness.

Jeremy reminded me of the time he called to ask how to cook a baked potato. That was years ago. Now he makes stuff with pancetta and prosciutto, so he's the star pupil.

Mary Ruth has three little children. Ruby is an energetic two-year-old, much like her mother. Mary Ruth often calls to share Ruby's latest escapade. (One involved potty training and a neighbor's white rug, but that's enough for you.)

She tells me Ruby's latest gig. I laugh and assure her they'll all turn into responsible adults. I tell her she'll probably never have to raise bail for Ruby, unless that neighbor with the white rug presses charges.

Not long ago, Jeremy called to ask me who the first president of Mexico was. The closest I came was Benito Juarez, but he wasn't president until 1855. When Jeremy hung up, I looked up Juarez and reminded myself of some Mexican history I had forgotten. My son is educational.

Recently, he called to ask how Spain's Franco managed to stay out of World War II, considering all the help he got from Hitler during the Spanish Civil War. Our reasoning was accurate and insightful and reminded me how bright my children are.

Sam just moved near Taos, New Mexico. He called last night to tell me about the haunted St. James Hotel in Cimarron, part of his new Sysco sales district. He had a history question about local shady characters, so I'll be brushing up on Western Americana now.

We have fun with phone calls, even if it's just to tell each other to study or clean house. We connect, and I'm secretly grateful they still think the old gal has information they want.

Wouldn't you know: As I was writing this, Liz called from Midland, Texas. She had to share a joke with her mum.

A panda walks into a bar and asks the bartender, "Do you have any . . . bamboo?"

"Sure," the bartender says, "but why the big pause?"
Says the panda, "It's not my fault. I was born with them."
My kids need me; I'm in heaven.

MARCH 29, 2007

CASH IN MY ATTIC

Did you read about the twins from Houston who found a 2.5-carat diamond at Crater of Diamonds State Park in Arkansas? The eight-year-olds were digging for diamonds, an activity encouraged by the park.

I'm a former National Park Service ranger who used to get all squinty-eyed when I noticed visitors toeing the ground at Fort Union Trading Post National Historic Site. Fort Union was an active trading post from 1828 to 1867. A lot of trade beads literally fell between the cracks. They still surface, and we discourage visitors from taking them home.

How do we do that? We do the "ranger mosey." In my case, it meant sauntering over to the perps while looking as casual as it's possible for a grandma in a uniform and Smokey the Bear hat to look.

I told them politely to stop, please, before I got really upset. "Really upset" meant no more campfire talks for them, and a sentence to a national park with surly bears and privies not emptied since before the Spanish-American War.

But here were these kids in Arkansas, digging away for six hours. Children like to dig. I could always tell when mine were trying to tunnel to China because all the spoons vanished from my silverware drawer. Either that, or southeast Wyoming was the Bermuda Triangle for cutlery.

The twins, Grace and Garrett Duncan, had unearthed a huge, light brown diamond. According to the article, a park interpreter grabbed it and ran into the superintendent's office, promising the twins she'd bring it back.

Yep, it was real. The twins had their gem mounted in a display case. With a fine sense of pride and humor, they've named it the Duncan Twins Diamond.

I never find anything, but I enjoy it when others do. Confession: my guilty pleasure television program is BBC's *Cash in the Attic*. It airs several times a week, and I watch when I can. Since I only discovered it a few months ago, even the reruns are fresh.

The premise: a team consisting of narrator and antique expert goes to the home of someone wanting to raise money for something or other. The team and family graze through the house, looking for items of value to sell at auction. Typically, families are trying to raise between £500 and £2,000 for their projects.

The thrill comes in the auction, where some "treasures" make diddly-squat, and others go through the roof, when two or more people bid against each other.

On the whole, British attics are possibly more exciting than American ones. Their country is older, and at least there is the potential for a greater antiques haul. The Duke of Wellington's shaving mirror is more likely to be found in Quagmire-on-Avon than in Dunseith, North Dakota.

My portable, US Navy childhood seems an unlikely time for antiques, but my folks had a doozy: a glass-front china cabinet that fit into a corner. The glass was at least four feet tall, and bowed out in front. It was beautiful.

Tough, too. We moved umpteen times—California to Georgia to Virginia to Texas to Alaska to California again. I don't remember it in Japan so maybe it was stored in the States.

In all those moves and more, that antique glass never shattered. My sister Wanda has the cabinet now. It's a piece of furniture worthy of any British auction.

We Kellys have one thing of value. At least, our older son wants it someday after I have croaked.

It's a big yellow Tupperware bowl. During the '70s, I was held hostage at a Tupperware party (why are they called parties?). The only way I could escape was to buy something.

I used the bowl a lot, back when the kids were home and I was cooking for what seemed like the Light Brigade, before it charged.

Mostly, though, it was the popcorn bowl. I wish I had a quarter for all the times it held popcorn. I'd quit my job tomorrow and retire to St. Simons Island, Georgia.

Jeremy wants that bowl. He loves popcorn. In his house in Sanderson,

Texas, he had a 50-pound sack of popcorn in his dining room. That's it. No furniture; just popcorn.

I'll give it to him, too, no auction involved. It's obviously of value to him. I don't foresee any bidding wars for the battered old thing, even if all it holds are popcorn and memories.

JULY 26, 2007

MAN'S MOST-FORGIVING FRIEND

I like to pretend I'm not overly sentimental, or prone to surprise. If you ever had any doubts, trust me: everything's been done. The preacher in Ecclesiastes was right—there is nothing new under the sun. Theoretically, nothing should surprise someone my age.

But, shucks, I'll admit I'm sentimental. Sometimes it catches me unaware and never more so than when I watched the movie *Eight Below*.

Maybe you saw it. The movie is based on what happened when a 1958 Japanese expedition to Antarctica was forced to abandon its sled dogs. When the Japanese returned months later, a few of their dogs were still alive, having survived what are arguably the worst conditions on earth. It was far worse than a North Dakota winter, stranded with only a DVD of *Pee-wee's Big Adventure*, or maybe a tape of "I've been to the desert on a horse with no name," on continuous loop.

You get the drift. The 2006 Disney version updates the story to 1993, when a guide at a US research base is forced to leave behind his eight dogs, with no prospect of rescue until Antarctica's long winter lifts.

Eight Below got solid reviews. I watched it recently.

Let me state here I don't like the cold. I thought *Dr. Zhivago* was a sappy movie because I couldn't wrap my mind around the idea of people too stupid to move to a warmer climate, for crying out loud (I was in Southern California at the time).

I don't like dogs, either. Big ones scare me and little ones look mostly ridiculous, especially when they think they're big dogs. This means you, all pugs and poms.

I am wary of those Husky, Samoyed, Malamute types. I spent a summer in the Aleutian Islands once, and never got over the creep factor of looking into the face of a dog with eyes bluer than mine. Tain't right.

Carla doesn't like snow much. She prefers cats to dogs. She claims she's not sentimental. Then why on earth was I sobbing like a fool through major portions of *Eight Below*?

Maybe it's because there's something heart wrenching about the trust animals and children have in grown-ups. Maybe they just naturally assume that adults are, well, more adult.

The guide, thinking the research team would make one more flight to save the dogs before winter clamped down, had staked them out as usual, and his Huskies trusted him. They hunkered down to wait. And wait. Old Jack died. The others finally broke free of their chains and somehow survived through a long, dark winter.

What happened to them during that time is purely speculative. The filmmakers were plausible in their suppositions, so it worked. The scenes flashed back and forth between the dogs as they soldiered on, and their guide in the US, anguished because he could not keep his promise.

I cried. I finally abandoned any pretense of dignity and just wallowed in my movie misery, worried about the dogs who—in their master's mind—had been betrayed.

There is one thing I like about dogs. In fact, it never ceases to amaze me. When the rescuers finally returned to Antarctica, there were the six surviving dogs, so gosh-darned grateful to see their frail, fallible humans and bearing not a single grudge.

Cats would never have done that. Any feline worth its catnip might have slooowly approached the rescuers, but it would have elaborately turned its back and sulked for another six months, give or take a year or two.

Not dogs. Not for nothing is there that prayer: "Lord, please make me the kind of person my dog thinks I am."

My sister Wanda and her husband were adopted by a mutt they named Fox. He's loyal. I'm sure it's old hat to my sis, but I'm always amused by Fox's eagerness when his humans return. His cup runneth over. He's in ecstasy, whether they've returned from two weeks in Egypt or down to the 7-11 for a Slurpee. If Fox could blow a trumpet, he would.

That's fine for some. I know my cat—the late, great Yoda—loved me. Recently, scientists have discovered that cats "kiss" by looking at their humans and slowly opening and closing their eyes. I wish I'd known that when Yoda was alive. I'd have had the good sense to repeat the gesture when Yoda did that to me.

AUGUST 21, 2007

GOT ZUCCHINI?

Have you noticed that August is the only month when people lock their cars in North Dakota? I discovered this when I tried to sneak a few zucchini into someone's backseat. No go. Where's that typical North Dakota compassion? I asked, indignant. Don't people care about the homeless?

Apparently not if they are homeless zucchini. Maybe everyone figures zucchini can forage for themselves during the warm months. For all I know, the Scenic Byway is lined with roving, feral zucchini, tossed out of car windows by desperate gardeners numb with the idea of thinking up one more way to disguise zucchini so folks will eat it.

My grandson likes fried zucchini, so I've sliced those little suckers, dunked them in batter, then done the hot oil thing, impervious to their tiny screams. I don't do it too often—not because I care much about pain inflicted on veggies—because I don't want Noah's arteries to slam shut before he reaches 14.

I've made zucchini bread, but after a while, that one cup of oil in the batter makes me cringe. Years ago when my own kids were small, I came across a recipe for faux pineapple, a.k.a. zucchini, dressed up in an itty bitty grass skirt with a flower tucked behind one ear. I didn't fool anyone. Come to think of it, maybe that was when my kids quit trusting me. Or maybe it was when I tried to disguise zucchini as Rice Krispie treats.

I'm certain I lost the trust of Noah's mom and his aunt when they were little girls and it started to rain one Halloween. I dressed them in green garbage bags and told them to go as zucchini. Honest. I only got away with that once, though, because they were young and still thought I knew what I was doing.

But here it is, August 2008, and I hear the sound of car doors locking all over town. In desperation, I went on the Internet. One website boasted

2,431 ways to use zucchini that didn't involve a catapult. I just couldn't face it.

I whined about this to Brenda, the sympathetic, talented woman who cuts my rapidly graying hair. She came up with an idea that was so good it was positively breathtaking and beats out any energy plan devised by any presidential candidate. According to Brenda, all we need to do is find a way to convert zucchini into gasoline.

I think I'm going to write in Brenda for president. She'll just turn this problem over to the fine agricultural minds at North Dakota State University, who will no doubt come up with a way to extract gasoline from zucchini. I mean, if we can get gasoline out of corn, why not zucchini?

Brenda is so cool. She could probably find a way to turn zucchini into cheap, affordable housing, so all those folks cast out by the home mortgage fiasco could have a little green roof over their heads. I mean, isn't there always at least one or two zucchinis that get overlooking every week and turn into behemoths the size of the Fargodome? Carve out a window or two, put some laminate flooring down in the kitchen and some berber in the living room, and presto! zucchini housing, without the hefty price tag.

Wouldn't you know it? With such a premium placed on their heretofore basically worthless existence, zucchini would probably organize and start making demands. There would be zucchini pride parades and public service announcements—clever, to be sure—about giving zucchini respect. Teachers would add a unit about zucchinis, so no zucchini would be left behind. Once zucchini started getting long-overdue respect, the floodgates would open for similar treatment of beets, radishes, and turnips, not to mention kohlrabi with a grudge. This could get out of hand, but we'll let another president worry about the potential mess. That's the time-honored solution.

In the meantime, I'll just avert my gaze from those pleading, zucchini eyes when I pass through the kitchen, and get the word out for all of us to write in Brenda's name in November. I'm counting on her.

Wait. Hold the phone. Brenda's way too smart to run for president. Maybe she could pass on her good ideas to the guys who do run. Once it's over, we can rest easy. Mission accomplished.

AUGUST 28, 2007

ZUCCHINI REDUX

I've already heard from the powerful zucchini lobby about last week's column. As you probably know, this is an influential lobby; to risk offending it is to court disaster of monumental proportions. In less than a week—zucchini protest about as fast as they grow—I've been threatened with the dire prospect of opening my fridge and seeing nothing in it but zucchini leering back. My favorite vegetables have already disappeared.

The lobby is also threatening to hold my oldest child for ransom. I'm not too concerned here, because he's a highly trained federal agent and is currently on a detail in another state which will remain nameless, but where people say, "Doncha know?" and "Fer neat" a lot. He has enough firepower to take down quite a few zucchini before he's sucked under.

Since I'm a wimp, I've agreed to give zucchini equal time. Still, as a founding member of Planet Grammaria, I have to wonder about the word, zucchini, itself. My extensive Latin language education—three years in high school. Can you top that, Father Schommer?—has me assuming that *zucchini* is plural. Is the singular of *zucchini* "zuccinus"? No, wait; there is no singular to *zucchini*. Have you ever seen just one?

Here it is. As part of my penance, I've agreed to print what is truly my favorite soup recipe in the world. It's made with—you guessed it—zucchini. My sister Wanda Lynn, who lives in that nameless, nearby state, made it a few years ago, and I appropriated it for home use in Nodak.

HEPBURN'S ZUCCHINI SOUP

¼ c. butter
2 pounds small zucchini, thinly sliced, not peeled
5 T. finely chopped shallots, or green onions (about 3)

Stop Me If You've Read This One

4 c. chicken broth
1½ tsp. curry powder
⅛ tsp. salt
⅛ tsp. cayenne pepper

Melt butter in large skillet. Add zucchini and shallots. Cover and cook 10–15 minutes, stirring often, until zucchini is soft, but not browned. Combine half of the zucchini mixture, 2 cups chicken broth and spices in food processor or blender. Puree. Pour into saucepan, if serving hot, or large bowl, if serving cold. Puree the other half of the ingredients. Combine batches. Serves 6.

I've been slicing zucchini and freezing it so I can make this soup in winter. I made it several times last winter, but what is more humiliating than having to *buy* zucchini in the store? It goes against everything I stand for (which obviously isn't much).

Zucchini reminds me of my favorite vegetable movie. It's called *Mr. Majestyk*, and stars Charles Bronson, world's best non-acting actor. He plays Vincent Majestyk, an ex-con, Vietnam vet who grows watermelon in southern Colorado. It's his last chance to get a good crop, but he ends up offending a hit man, and the mob is out to get him. Throughout the story, all Vince Majestyk wants to do is bring in his melon crop.

The movie is full of baddies. Family favorite is Bobby Kopas, played by Paul Koslo. Kopas is a small-time punk who ends up irritating both sides. He also has perpetual bad hair. The guys can't catch a break. He also gets one of the movie's great lines directed at him: Mr. Majestyk to Koslo—"You make sounds like you're a mean little a**-kicker." That line has gone into family legend. All anyone has to do is say, "You make sounds . . ." and we get the picture.

My whole family loves this movie. We've seen it a gazillion times, and most of us own it on DVD. I've already told my kids that for our 50th wedding anniversary, we're gonna put in the DVD, turn off the sound, and do all the dialog ourselves.

The greatest scene? Vince has harvested all the watermelons and they're stored in a big shed. The mob shows up with AK47s or Kalashnikovs and, just to rile ol' Vince, proceed to shoot up his crop. Before the violence starts, the hit man says, "You heard what the man said. Let's bring in his melons." What a super scene: all those defenseless watermelons being blasted to bits.

You'd never see anything like that with zucchini. Not zucchini; they wouldn't go gentle into that good night, no siree. They're almost as tough as Charles Bronson.

There it is. You have my favorite soup recipe and my favorite guilty pleasure movie. Zucchini rules. Or is that, zucchinis rule? Beats me. "I make sounds . . ."

ABOUT THE AUTHOR

Carla Kelly is a veteran of the New York and international publishing world. The author of more than thirty novels and novellas for Donald I. Fine Co., Signet, and Harlequin, Carla is the recipient of two RITA Awards (think Oscars for romance writing) from Romance Writers of America and two Spur Awards (think Oscars for western fiction) from Western Writers of America.

Recently, she's been writing Regency romances (think *Pride and Prejudice*) set in the Royal Navy's Channel Fleet during the Napoleonic Wars between England and France. She comes by her love of the ocean from her childhood as a Navy brat.

Photo by Marie Bryner-Bowles, Bryner Photography

Carla's history background makes her no stranger to footnote work, either. During her National Park Service days at the Fort Union Trading Post National Historic Site, Carla edited Friedrich Kurz's fur trade journal. She recently completed a short history of Fort Buford, where Sitting Bull surrendered in 1881.

Following the "dumb luck" principle that has guided their lives, the Kellys recently moved to Wellington, Utah, from North Dakota and couldn't be happier in their new location. In her spare time, Carla volunteers at the Railroad and Mining Museum in Helper, Utah. She likes to visit her five children, who live here and there around the United States. Her favorite place in Utah is Manti, located after a drive on the scenic byway through Huntington Canyon.

And why is she so happy these days? Carla doesn't have to write in laundry rooms and furnace rooms now, because she has an actual office.